MW00577848

.

▶ Translanguaging

DOI: 10.1057/9781137385765

Other Palgrave Pivot titles

DOI: 10.1057/9781137385765

palgrave▸pivot

Translanguaging: Language, Bilingualism and Education

Ofelia García
The Graduate Center, City University of New York, USA

and

Li Wei
Birkbeck College, University of London, UK

DOI: 10.1057/9781137385765

First published 2014 by
PALGRAVE MACMILLAN

Palgrave Macmillan in the UK is an imprint of Macmillan Publishers Limited, registered in England, company number 785998, of Houndmills, Basingstoke, Hampshire RG21 6XS.

Palgrave Macmillan in the US is a division of St Martin's Press LLC, 175 Fifth Avenue, New York, NY 10010.

Palgrave Macmillan is the global academic imprint of the above companies and has companies and representatives throughout the world.

Palgrave® and Macmillan® are registered trademarks in the United States, the United Kingdom, Europe and other countries.

ISBN: 978-1-137-38576-5 PDF
ISBN: 978-1-349-48138-5

A catalogue record for this book is available from the British Library.

A catalog record for this book is available from the Library of Congress.

www.palgrave.com/pivot

DOI: 10.1057/9781137385765

To our families

who have taught us about the possibilities of hope and love in translanguaging.

DOI: 10.1057/9781137385765

Contents

DOI: 10.1057/9781137385765

DOI: 10.1057/9781137385765

List of Figures

DOI: 10.1057/9781137385765

List of Tables

▶

Acknowledgments

We would like to thank the following persons for their reading of the manuscript and their helpful observations: Cecilia Espinosa, Nelson Flores, Sarah Hesson, Zhu Hua, Kate Seltzer and Zohar Eviatar. We are also grateful to Alisa Algava for her help with the references and to Heather Woodley for her help with the Figures. Some of the examples are drawn from different projects in the UK and the USA. In the UK, examples are drawn from 'Investigating multilingualism in complementary schools in four communities', funded by the Economic and Social Research Council, UK (RES-000-23-1180), and 'Translation and translanguaging: Investigating linguistic and cultural transformations in superdiverse wards in four UK cities', funded by the Arts and Humanities Research Council, UK (AH/L007096/1). Angela Creese, Adrian Blackledge, Mike Baynham, Zhu Hua and Vally Lytra who worked on these and other projects together with Li Wei have provided invaluable input into the ideas that are expressed in this book. In the US, examples are drawn from the project 'Latinos in New York High School', funded by the New York City Office of English Language Learners, the 'PAIHS Study', funded by the International Network for Public High Schools and the CUNY-NYSIEB Project, funded by the New York State Education Department, under the initiative of Arlen Benjamin-Gómez. The dialogue of García with the large CUNY-NYSIEB team who are identified in note 1, Chapter 7, and above all with the Principal Investigator, Ricardo Otheguy, *colega y compañero entrañable en la vida,* has enriched the understandings of translanguaging that are reflected in this book.

DOI: 10.1057/9781137385765

Introduction

Abstract: *The short introduction poses the main question of the book: What is translanguaging? What does a translanguaging approach mean for language and bilingualism on the one hand, and for education and bilingual education on the other? It also describes the structure of the book – Part I discusses how traditional understandings of language and bilingualism are transformed through a translanguaging lens, and Part II explores how translanguaging alters traditional understandings of education.*

Keywords: translanguaging

García, Ofelia, and Li Wei. *Translanguaging: Language, Bilingualism and Education.* Basingstoke: Palgrave Macmillan, 2014. DOI: 10.1057/9781137385765.

What is *translanguaging*? What does a translanguaging approach mean for language and bilingualism on the one hand, and for education and bilingual education on the other? We attempt here to answer the question of how translanguaging shapes our understandings of *language*, and the concomitant concepts of *bilingualism, multilingualism* and *plurilingualism*, as well as our theories and practices of education, especially of *bilingual education*.[1] As we will see, for us translanguaging is an approach to the use of language, bilingualism and the education of bilinguals that considers the language practices of bilinguals not as two autonomous language systems as has been traditionally the case, but as one linguistic repertoire with features that have been societally constructed as belonging to two separate languages.

We start in Part I of this book by reviewing the ways in which language was conceptualized in the 20th century and the epistemological changes that are taking place as global interactions, real and virtual, define our language exchanges in what Vertovec has called 'super-diversity' (2007) and May (2013) has referred to as 'the multilingual turn'.[2] In so doing, we introduce the concept of *languaging*, an important part of the term trans-*languaging* that we explore here. We also review the ways in which bilingualism, plurilingualism and multilingualism have been conceptualized traditionally in the past, and we consider how the trans-lens of *trans*-languaging alters our common understandings of bilingualism. Many scholars have proposed alternative terms to bilingualism, multilingualism and plurilingualism, and we review those here, as we describe what they have in common and what distinguishes them from our use of translanguaging.

In Part II of this book, we review traditional understandings of education, and especially of bilingual education; that is, educational efforts to develop children's plurilingual abilities or to use those abilities to educate bilingual students. We then consider how scholars have used translanguaging in educational contexts, and how a translanguaging lens has the potential to transform structures and practices of educating bilingually, which would have implications to change society.

The emphasis on the 'trans' aspects of language *and* education enables us to transgress the categorical distinctions of the past. In particular, a 'trans' approach to language and education liberates our traditional understandings and points to three innovative aspects in considering language on the one hand, and education on the other, that we will develop in this book:

DOI: 10.1057/9781137385765

1 Referring to a *trans-system and trans-spaces*; that is, to fluid practices that go *between* and *beyond* socially constructed language and educational systems, structures and practices to engage diverse students' multiple meaning-making systems and subjectivities.

2 Referring to its *trans-formative nature*; that is, as new configurations of language practices and education are generated, old understandings and structures are released, thus transforming not only subjectivities[3], but also cognitive and social structures. In so doing, orders of discourses shift and the voices of Others come to the forefront, relating then translanguaging to criticality, critical pedagogy, social justice and the linguistic human rights agenda.

3 Referring to the *trans-disciplinary* consequences of the languaging *and* education analysis, providing a tool for understanding not only language practices on the one hand and education on the other, but also human sociality, human cognition and learning, social relations and social structures.

In Part I, we trace the development of the shift from language to languaging and the emergence of the concept of translanguaging.

Notes

1 When speaking about language, we include the concepts of *bilingualism, multilingualism* and *plurilingualism*. When referring to education, however, we speak about *bilingual education* to recognize specific educational efforts to develop children's plurilingual abilities or to use those abilities to educate. We thus use bilingual education as an umbrella term to encompass what is also called trilingual and multilingual education, while recognizing that the bi- does not, in this case, refer to two, but to complex linguistic interactions that cannot be enumerated. We also recognize that most classrooms in today's globalized world are multilingual, but in speaking about bilingual education, we're focusing here on the complex language practices that enable the education of students with plurilingual abilities.

2 We recognize that these fluid language exchanges existed even prior to the modern era, as Canagarajah (2013) has evidenced.

3 We speak about subjectivities, and not identities that point to an inner stable core. Subjectivities reflect the post-structuralist position of processes through which outside forces make us a changing subject and imbue our position within ideologies.

DOI: 10.1057/9781137385765

Part I
Language and Translanguaging

▶

DOI: 10.1057/9781137385765

1
Language, Languaging and Bilingualism

Abstract: *This first chapter explores the shifts that have recently taken place as traditional understandings of language and bilingualism are transformed. After reflecting on views of language, the chapter introduces the concept of languaging, and follows its emergence among scholars and as it has developed in the sociolinguistic and psycholinguistic literature. The chapter then reviews traditional concepts of bilingualism, multilingualism and plurilingualism as they have been studied from monolingual perspectives that view them only as double- or many-monolingualisms. It then reviews more dynamic views of these phenomena, arguing that to capture this complexity more is needed than the term languaging. It proposes translanguaging as a way to capture the fluid language practices of bilinguals without giving up the social construction of language and bilingualism under which speakers operate.*

Keywords: bilingualism; languaging; multilingualism; plurilingualism; psycholinguistics; sociolinguistics; translanguaging

García, Ofelia, and Li Wei. *Translanguaging: Language, Bilingualism and Education.* Basingstoke: Palgrave Macmillan, 2014. DOI: 10.1057/9781137385765.

Reflecting on language

To most people, language is what we speak, hear, read or write in everyday life. And we speak, hear, read and write in what are considered different languages, such as Arabic, Chinese, Spanish and Urdu. In the theoretical discipline of Linguistics, however, tensions and controversies abound as to how language is conceptualized. One of the founding fathers of modern linguistics, the Swiss linguist Ferdinand de Saussure, famously described language as a system of signs. Moreover, linguistic signs are arbitrary, that is, a linguistic sign is an association between a sound image and a concept, and the sound-meaning association is established by arbitrary convention for each language. This conventionality accounts for the diversity of languages. Following this line of argument, for example, early 20th-century structural linguists demonstrated how, historically, cultural assumptions informed the development of such structures as word orders, gender morphologies and event reporting in different languages.

Saussure's ideas of signs and the relationship between the signifier and the signified gave rise to the field of *semiotics*, the study of signs and sign processes, and the acknowledgment of the social dimensions of language. But within Linguistics, his insistence that language could be analyzed as a formal system of differential elements, apart from the messy dialectics of real-time production and comprehension, and in particular, his distinction between *langue*, the abstract rules and conventions of a signifying system independent of individual users on the one hand, and *parole*, the concrete instances of the use of *langue* by individuals in a series of speech acts on the other, led to the divergence of interests in two very different directions. One trend pursued universal structures across human languages; the other followed how human beings put to use their linguistic knowledge in real-life contexts.

Noam Chomsky refashioned the *langue* versus *parole* distinction in terms of *competence* versus *performance*, the former referring to the tacit knowledge of the language system and the latter, the use of language in concrete situations. For Chomsky, Linguistics should be concerned with what all languages have in common, what he called Universal Grammar (UG). Yet, the goal of the UG enterprise is to abstract away from the diversity, the details and the plurality of human languages. In fact, Chomsky (1995: 54) suggests that the main task of linguistic theory 'is to show that the…diversity of linguistic phenomena is illusory'. There is an inherent problem with

DOI: 10.1057/9781137385765

Chomsky's logic, as Burton-Roberts (2004) points out. That is, if UG is supposed to be about all languages as Chomsky seems to want it to be, then it cannot be conceptualized as a natural, biological, genetic endowment, as particular languages, as we know them (e.g. Arabic, Chinese, English, Spanish), are historically evolved social conventions; and if UG is about something entirely natural, biological or genetic, then it cannot be a theory of actual languages that human beings use in society. But the main issue we have with Chomsky's line of inquiry is that he sets the discipline of Linguistics against the reality of linguistic diversity, a historical fact that has been further enhanced by the globalization of contemporary society.

Mikhail Bakhtin's formulation of *heteroglossia* in the early 20th century challenged the structuralist conception of language by Saussure and the strictly mentalist conception of Chomsky, both of whom removed language from context of use. Bakhtin posited that language is inextricably bound to the context in which it exists and is incapable of neutrality because it emerges from the actions of speakers with certain perspective and ideological positioning. To make an utterance, says Bakhtin, means to take language over, 'shot through with intentions and accents' (as cited in Morris, 1994: 293). Another close associate of Bakhtin after the Russian revolution was Valentin Nikolaevic Vološinov, a Marxist philosopher of language, who strongly supported Bakhtin's dialogic position on language. Language, Vološinov says, acquires life 'in concrete verbal communication, and not in the abstract linguistic system of language forms, nor in the individual psyche of speakers' (1929/1973: 95). A shift was occurring that led to the coining of the term 'languaging'.

The emergence of languaging

Perhaps the first scholars to talk about 'languaging' were not linguists but the Chilean biologists Humberto Maturana and Francisco Varela who in 1973 posited their theory of *autopoeisis*. Autopoeisis argues that we cannot separate our biological and social history of actions from the ways in which we perceive the world. Our experience, Maturana and Varela say, is moored to our structure in a binding way, and the processes involved in our makeup, in our actions as human beings, constitute our knowledge. What is known is brought forth through action and practice, and is not simply based on acquiring the relevant features of a pre-given world that can be decomposed into significant fragments. As Maturana and

DOI: 10.1057/9781137385765

Varela (1998: 26) say: 'All doing is knowing, and all knowing is doing'. Their autopoeisis view of biological life leads to their observations about language:

> It is by *languaging* that the act of knowing, in the behavioral coordination which is language, brings forth a world. We work out our lives in a *mutual linguistic coupling*, not because language permits us to reveal ourselves but because we are constituted in language in a *continuous becoming that we bring forth with others*. (1998: 234–235, italics added)

Language is not a simple system of structures that is independent of human actions with others, of our being with others. The term *languaging* is needed to refer to the simultaneous process of continuous becoming of ourselves and of our language practices, as we interact and make meaning in the world.

Another scholar who early on used the term 'languaging' was A. L. Becker. Writing about translation, Becker (1988) further posited that language is not simply a code or a system of rules or structures; rather what he calls *languaging* shapes our experiences, stores them, retrieves them and communicates them in an open-ended process. Languaging both shapes and is shaped by context. Becker (1995) explains: 'All languaging is what in Java is called *jarwa dhosok*, taking old language (*jarwa*) and pushing (*dhosok*) it into new contexts' (185). For Becker, language can never be accomplished; and thus *languaging* is a better term to capture an ongoing process that is always being created as we interact with the world lingually. To learn a new way of languaging is not just to learn a new code, Becker says, it is to enter another history of interactions and cultural practices and to learn 'a new way of being in the world' (1995: 227). In appealing to the concept of languaging, Becker is shaping what he calls 'a linguistics of particularity' (1988: 21) within the Humanities.

Using Becker's definition of languaging, the Argentinean semiotician Walter Mignolo (2000) reminds us that language is not a fact, a system of syntactic, semantic and phonetic rules. Rather, Mignolo says, *languaging* is 'thinking and writing between languages' and 'speech and writing are strategies for orienting and manipulating social domains of interaction' (226). Mignolo's reference to 'manipulation' reminds us that all languaging is enmeshed in systems of power, and thus, can be oppressive or liberating, depending on the positioning of speakers and their agency.

DOI: 10.1057/9781137385765

Languaging, sociolinguistics and psycholinguistics

New patterns of global activity characterized by intensive flows of people, capital goods and discourses have been experienced since the late 20th century. These have been driven by new technologies, as well as by a neoliberal economy that with its emphasis on the marketization of life has destabilized old social and economic structures and produced new forms of global inequalities. With interactions increasingly occurring in what Mary Louise Pratt (1991) refers to as 'contact zones' (often virtual ones) between speakers of different origins, experiences and characteristics, language is less and less understood as a monolithic autonomous system made up of discrete structures (as in Saussure) or a context-free mental grammar (as in Chomsky). We have entered 'a new way of being in the world' (Becker, 1995: 227), a world with Other spaces that are neither here nor there in a *heterotopia* as Foucault (1986) has called them.

With the rise of post-structuralism in the post-modern era, language has begun to be conceptualized as a *series of social practices and actions* by speakers that are embedded in a web of social *and* cognitive relations. Furthermore, a critique of nation-state/colonial language ideologies has emerged, seeking to excavate subaltern knowledge (Canagarajah, 2005; Flores, 2012, 2013; Makoni and Makoni, 2010; Makoni and Pennycook, 2007; Mignolo, 2000; Pennycook, 2010; Rosa, 2010). Post-structuralist critical language scholars treat language as contested space – as tools that are re-appropriated by actual language users. Ultimately, the goal of these critiques is to break out of static conceptions of language that keep power in the hands of the few, thus embracing the fluid nature of actual and local language practices of all speakers (Flores, 2013; Flores and García, 2013). The focus on language practices of language users has been signaled by the adoption of the term *languaging* by many sociolinguists (Canagarajah, 2007; Jørgensen and Juffermans, 2011; Juffermans, 2011; Makoni and Pennycook, 2007; Møller and Jørgensen, 2009; Shohamy, 2006), emphasizing the agency of speakers in an ongoing process of interactive meaning-making.

These new ways of being in the world have produced alternative understandings of the sociolinguistics of globalization; languages are *mobile resources* or practices within social, cultural, political and historical contexts (Blommaert, 2010). Languages are seen by post-structuralist sociolinguists as 'a product of the deeply social and cultural activities in which people engage' (Pennycook, 2010: 1) with meanings created through

DOI: 10.1057/9781137385765

ideological systems situated within historical moments (Foucault, 1972). Pennycook (2010) adds: 'To look at language as a practice is to view language as an activity rather than a structure, as something we do rather than a system we draw on, as a material part of social and cultural life rather than an abstract entity' (2). That is, language is seen neither as a system of structures nor a product located in the mind of speaker. What we have is languaging, 'a social process constantly reconstructed in sensitivity to environmental factors' (Canagarajah, 2007: 94). Shohamy (2006) uses the term 'languaging' to refer to 'language as an integral and natural component of interaction, communication and construction of meaning' (2). We are all *languagers* who use semiotic resources at our disposal in strategic ways to communicate and act in the world, but which are recognized by the bilingual speaker, as well as by others, as belonging to two sets of socially constructed 'languages'. Thus, Jørgensen and Juffermans (2011) refer to the human turn in sociolinguistics, by which the traditional Fishmanian question 'who speaks (or writes) what language (or what language variety) to whom, when and to what end' becomes '*who languages how and what is being languaged under what circumstances in a particular place and time*' (Juffermans, 2011: 165). The human turn in sociolinguistics, Juffermans argues, is 'toward language (in singular or as a verb) as a sociolinguistic system that is constructed and inhabited by people' (165).

As sociolinguists have become more interested in the cognitive side of language practices, psycholinguists are also considering the social aspects of cognitive engagement (e.g. see studies in Cook and Bassetti, 2011; Javier, 2007; Pavlenko, 2006). Thus, post-structuralist psycholinguists have also referred to languaging as 'a process of using language to gain knowledge, to make sense, to articulate one's thought and to communicate about using language' (Li Wei, 2011b: 1224). That is, the focus is on the speaker's *creative and critical use* of linguistic resources to mediate cognitively complex activities (Swain and Deters, 2007). As Swain has said, languaging 'serves as a vehicle through which thinking is articulated and transformed into an artifactual form' (Swain, 2000: 97). This is consistent with Cook's notion of *multicompetence* (Cook, 2012; Cook and Li Wei, forthcoming), which focuses on the intertwining of language and cognition: multicompetence is not confined to the language aspects of the mind but is also linked to cognitive processes and concepts. This means, on the one hand, not putting barriers between language and other cognitive systems, and on the other, denying the no-language

DOI: 10.1057/9781137385765

position that language is simply an artifact of other cognitive processes. Extending Maturana and Varela (1973), all languaging is knowing and doing, and all knowing and doing is languaging.

One of the differences between the orientations of post-structuralist sociolinguists and psycholinguists with regards to *languaging* is that whereas sociolinguists focus on the context of use of languaging, psycholinguists look at languaging as the property of individuals, not situations; although recently Cook, for instance, has extended his notion of multicompetence to communities as well (see, e.g. Cook, 2012; also Brutt-Griffler, 2002). Regardless of the difference, the emphasis on languaging today by both sociolinguists and psycholinguists extends our traditional understandings of languages. The next section discusses bilingualism and related phenomena, while starting to ponder how languaging further impacts our understandings of bilingualism.

Bilingualism, multilingualism, plurilingualism

It was the Saussurean vision of language as a self-contained system of structures that permeated the vision of language in early studies of bilingualism. Haugen (1956) gave an early definition of the term *bilingual*: 'Bilingual is a cover term for people with a number of different language skills, having in common only that they are not monolingual.... [A] bilingual... is one who knows two languages, but will here be used to include also the one who knows more than two, variously known as a plurilingual, a multilingual, or a polyglot' (9). Uriel Weinreich (1974) provided a similar definition: 'The practice of alternately using two languages will be called bilingualism, and the persons involved, bilingual' (1). *Bilingual* has thus come to mean knowing and using two autonomous languages. The term *multilingual* is often used to mean knowing and using more than two languages. The Council of Europe has proposed that the term *plurilingual* be reserved for the individual's 'ability to use several languages to varying degrees and for distinct purposes' (2000: 168), whereas the term *multilingual* be used only in relationship to the many languages of societal groups and not of individuals.

Despite their different emphases, the terms bilingualism, multilingualism and plurilingualism have one thing in common – they refer to a plurality of autonomous languages, whether two (bilingual) or many (multilingual), at the individual (bilingual/plurilingual) or societal level

DOI: 10.1057/9781137385765

(multilingual), and do not suggest the concept of 'languaging' presented above. Traditional notions of bilingualism and multilingualism are *additive,* that is, speakers are said to 'add up' whole autonomous languages or even partial structural bits of these languages (as in the Council of Europe's concept of plurilingualism). When societies and classrooms are said to be bilingual or multilingual, what is meant is that people in these places speak more than one language. There are also more extreme positions by some theoretical linguists, who, following Chomsky, believe that a speaker has a set of mini-grammars for different lexical domains, leading to different representations in the speaker's mind. Bilingualism is then understood as the representation of these mini-grammars, hence the term Universal Bilingualism (Roeper, 1999).

Bilingualism as dual

Precisely because of the structural treatment of languages as separate codes with different structures, the literature on bilingualism points to the problems 'of keeping the two languages apart' (Haugen, 1956: 155). Weinreich (1953: 1), an early scholar of bilingualism, talks about 'linguistic interference' as 'deviations from the norm of either language that occur in the speech of bilinguals as a result of their familiarity with more than one language'. The linguist's task is then defined as identifying all cases of interference resulting from language contact. For example, the process of code-switching, that is, what has been defined as going back and forth from one language belonging to one grammatical system to another, has received much attention in the literature on bilingualism (see, e.g. Auer, 1999; Myers-Scotton, 1993). Code-switching behavior is often stigmatized, although recent research has questioned this deficit orientation (see, among others, Auer, 2005; Zentella, 1997). In psycholinguistics and neurolinguistics, language differentiation of bilingual speakers has been made into a core research issue for laboratory investigations. Different languages are said to be represented by different neural networks in the bilingual brain, resulting in differential access in speech production (Costa and Santesteban, 2004; Fabbro, 2001; Goral, Levy, Obler and Cohen, 2006; Kim, Relkin, Lee and Hirsch, 1997). There is a preoccupation by experimental designers to focus on the ability to distinguish and separate languages as a telltale performance indicator of a bilingual's linguistic proficiency, even competence (Bosch and Sebastian-Galles, 1997; Dijkstra and Van Heuven, 2002). And a great

DOI: 10.1057/9781137385765

deal of effort has been made in search of a biologically rooted 'language switch' in code-switching that would actually signal when a separate language comes on (Hernández, Dapretto, Mazziotta and Bookheimer, 2001; Hernández, 2009).

Early in the study of bilingualism, Cummins (1979) posited that the proficiency of bilinguals in two languages was not stored separately in the brain, and that each proficiency did not behave independently of the other. With the concept of the Common Underlying Proficiency (CUP) explained through the image of the dual iceberg, Cummins proposed that although on the surface the structural elements of the two languages might look different, there is a cognitive *interdependence* that allows for transfer of linguistic practices. More recently, neurolinguistic studies of bilinguals have confirmed, and gone beyond, Cummins's hypothesis, showing that even when one language is being used, the other language remains active and can be easily accessed (Dijkstra, Van Jaarsveld and Ten Brinke, 1998; Hoshino and Thierry, 2011; Thierry et al., 2009; Wu and Thierry, 2010). Research on cognition and multilingual functioning has also supported the view that the 'languages' of bilingual speakers inter-act collaboratively in listening or speaking (De Groot, 2011). The view of bilingualism as simply dual is beginning to shift to a more dynamic one.

Bilingualism as dynamic

Grosjean (1982) argued that bilinguals are not two monolinguals in one person. Heller (2007) then debunked the concept of bilingualism as two autonomous languages and defined it as,

> sets of resources called into play by social actors, under social and historical conditions which both constrain and make possible the social reproduc-tion of existing conventions and relations, as well as the production of new ones. (15)

Heller's definition pays attention to ideologies surrounding language and moves us towards *processes* surrounding our languaging.

Related to Cummins's view of linguistic interdependence, but squarely centered on more integrative sociolinguistic practices as in Heller, and not on mentalist definitions of proficiency, García (2009a) proposed that bilingualism is *dynamic*, and not just additive, as had been conceptual-ized by Wallace Lambert in 1974. Unlike the view of two separate systems that are added (or even interdependent), a dynamic conceptualization of bilingualism goes beyond the notion of two autonomous languages,

DOI: 10.1057/9781137385765

of a first language (L1) and a second language (L2), and of additive or subtractive bilingualism. Instead, dynamic bilingualism suggests that the language *practices* of bilinguals are complex and interrelated; they do not emerge in a linear way or function separately since there is only one linguistic system. Dynamic bilingualism goes beyond the idea that there are two languages that are interdependent as in Cummins (1979); instead, it connotes one linguistic system that has features that are most often practiced according to societally constructed and controlled 'languages', but other times producing new practices. Figure 1.1 delineates this difference between traditional understandings of bilingualism, those of Cummins's interdependence and those of dynamic bilingualism.

In Figure 1.1, the view of traditional bilingualism is rendered by two separate rectangles that represent two languages and separate linguistic systems (an L1 and an L2) with different linguistic features (F1 and F2). The Linguistic Interdependence proposed by Cummins is depicted in Figure 1.1 by bringing closer the two linguistic systems and proposing that there is transfer between the two, stemming from a Common Underlying Proficiency (depicted by the rectangle below), but still delineating separate L1 and L2 and separate linguistic features. The Dynamic

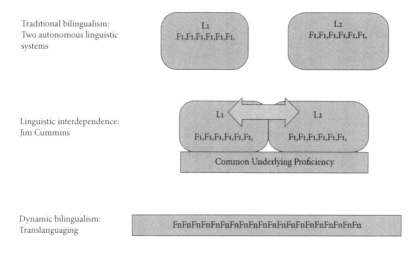

Traditional bilingualism:
Two autonomous linguistic
systems

Linguistic interdependence:
Jim Cummins

Dynamic bilingualism:
Translanguaging

*L = Linguistic system
F = Linguistic feature

FIGURE 1.1   *Difference between views of traditional bilingualism, linguistic interdependence and dynamic bilingualism*

DOI: 10.1057/9781137385765

Bilingual Model that is related to our theories of translanguaging (which will be the subject of the next chapter) posits that there is but one linguistic system (rendered in Figure 1.1 by one rectangle) with features that are integrated (Fn) throughout. Not depicted in the figure is the fact that these linguistic features are then, as we said before, often used in ways that conform to societal constructions of 'a language', and at other times used differently.

In general, our position is compatible with the *language-mode* perspective favored by Grosjean (2004), though it differs from it in one important respect. In their recent analysis of Hispanic bilingualism, García and Otheguy (forthcoming) explain:

> With Grosjean, we see bilinguals selecting features from their linguistic repertoire depending on contextual, topical, and interactional factors. But we do not follow Grosjean when he defines a language mode as 'a state of activation of the bilingual's languages and language-processing mechanisms' (2004: 40). In our conception, there are no two languages that are cognitively activated or deactivated as the social and contextual situation demands, but rather, as we have proposed, a single array of disaggregated features that is always activated.

The process by which bilingual speakers engage in order to select the societally appropriate features to conform to contextual, topical and interactional factors is related to Althusser's concept of *interpellation* (1972), the idea that institutions and their discourses call us, or hail us, into particular identities through the ideologies they shape. Societal forces, and in particular schools, enforce a call, an interpellation, by which bilingual speakers are often able to recognize themselves only as subjects that speak two separate languages. In so doing, bilingual speakers become complicit in their own domination as they often conform to monolingual monoglossic practices that constrain their own bilingualism to two separate autonomous languages, although at times they may resist by engaging in fluid language practices. The interpellation of bilingual subjects in societies that view languages as separate systems requires that speakers act 'monolingually' at times. But this does not mean that bilinguals possess two language systems. In effect, the research by Bialystok, Craik, Klein and Viswanathan (2004) suggests that it is the constant use of the bilinguals' brain Executive Control System in having to sort through the language features that gives bilinguals a cognitive advantage.

DOI: 10.1057/9781137385765

As García (2009a) has said, dynamic bilingual practices do not result in either the balanced wheels of two bicycles (as in the concept of additive bilingualism) or in a unicycle (as in the concept of subtractive bilingualism). Instead dynamic bilingualism is like an all-terrain vehicle (ATV) with individuals using their entire linguistic repertoire to adapt to both the ridges and craters of communication in uneven (and unequal) interactive terrains (see García, 2009a; García and Kleifgen, 2010), and to the confines of language use as controlled by societal forces, especially in schools. García (2009a) uses the image of a banyan tree to capture the reality of dynamic bilingualism. Banyan trees start their lives when seeds germinate in the cracks and crevices of a host tree and send down roots towards the ground which envelop the host tree, also growing horizontal roots. These horizontal roots then fuse with the descending ones and girdle the tree, sometimes becoming the 'columnar tree' when the host tree dies. Dynamic bilingualism emerges in the same way, in the cracks and crevices of communication with others who language differently, gradually becoming in and of itself a way of languaging through complex communicative interactions. Dynamic bilingualism is then both the foundation of languaging and the goal for communication in an increasingly multilingual world (see also Clyne, 2003).

Beyond and with bilingualism: transformations

Psycholinguists have also recently proposed that the co-adaptation of language resources in multilingual interactions is related to psychologically and sociologically determined communicative needs, while suggesting that language resources are thus transformed. To become bilingual is then not just the 'taking in' of linguistic forms by learners, but 'the constant adaptation of their linguistic resources in the service of meaning-making in response to the affordances that emerge in the communicative situation, which is, in turn, affected by learners' adaptability' (Larsen-Freeman and Cameron, 2008: 135). In so doing, the language-using patterns affect the whole system, as they generate emergent languaging patterns. A Dynamic Systems Theory allows us to reconcile psycholinguistics with sociolinguistics, offering an integrative approach. As Larsen-Freeman and Cameron (2008) explain:

> A complex systems approach takes a view of the individual's cognitive processes as inextricably interwoven with their experiences in the physical and social world. The context of language activity is socially constructed

DOI: 10.1057/9781137385765

and often dynamically negotiated on a moment-by-moment basis. (155, emphasis added)

Dynamic Systems Theory (Herdina and Jessner, 2002) holds that there is interaction between internal cognitive ecosystems and external social ecosystems; thus, languaging is always being co-constructed between humans and their environments. A translanguaging approach, as we will see later, relates to this position of Dynamic Systems Theory, although it insists on transforming, not simply dismissing, the concept of bilingualism.

In a convincing book, Makoni and Pennycook (2007) have debunked the concept of a language, arguing that the idea of a language is a European invention, a product of colonialism and of a Herderian 19th-century nationalist romanticist ideology that insisted that language and identity were intrinsically linked. Makoni and Pennycook (2007) state:

> Languages do not exist as real entities in the world and neither do they emerge from or represent real environments; they are, by contrast, the inventions of social, cultural and political movements. (2)

But Makoni and Pennycook (2007) also insist on dismissing the concepts of bilingualism, plurilingualism and multilingualism because they reproduce 'the same concept of language that underpins all mainstream linguistic thought' (22). Just as the concept of language needs 'disinvention', separate languages with different labels, given by linguists and others but often unknown and unused by their speakers, are questioned as serving nation-state interests (Makoni and Pennycook, 2007). English is regarded as a language only in comparison with the existence of other languages such as French, Spanish or Chinese. None of these languages exist on their own, and all languages are in contact with others – being influenced by others, and containing structural elements from others. As Canagarajah (2013) says: 'To turn Chomsky (1988) on his head, we are all translinguals, not native speakers of a single language in homogenous environments' (8). Moreover, national 'languages' are constituted with resources from diverse places and times. Thus, Makoni and Pennycook propose that 'languaging' might be a sufficient term to capture plural linguistic practices. Our position, however, on the question of bilingualism is different. We think that a term other than just 'languaging' is needed to refer to complex multilingual situations. As Hall, Cheng and Carlson (2006) have said: 'multilinguals' amount and diversity of experience and use go beyond that of monolinguals' (229).

DOI: 10.1057/9781137385765

Multilinguals can also draw on 'more modalities of signification than one single symbolic system' (Kramsch, 2009: 99). Mignolo (2000: 229) reminds us: 'You may or may not have a "mother tongue" as Derrida argues, but you cannot avoid "being born" in one or more language(s), to have them inscribed in your body.'

We argue that the term *translanguaging* offers a way of capturing the expanded complex practices of speakers who could not avoid having had languages inscribed in their body, and yet live between different societal and semiotic contexts as they interact with a complex array of speakers. A translanguaging approach to bilingualism extends the repertoire of semiotic practices of individuals and transforms them into dynamic mobile resources that can adapt to global and local sociolinguistic situations. At the same time, translanguaging also attends to the social construction of language and bilingualism under which speakers operate. It is to a more extended discussion of translanguaging that we now turn.

DOI: 10.1057/9781137385765

2

The Translanguaging Turn and Its Impact

Abstract: *This chapter traces the development of a translanguaging theory from its origins in Wales. It draws differences between translanguaging and code-switching, describes it as the discursive norm among bilinguals, and considers the speakers' construction of a translanguaging space. The chapter also looks at the relationship of translanguaging to Dynamic Systems Theory, to multimodalities and to writing. Finally, the chapter considers the contributions of translanguaging to Linguistics theory and the concept of linguistic creativity. The chapter ends by reviewing concepts and terms that have recently proliferated to emphasize the more fluid language practices of bilingual speakers and to relate and differentiate translanguaging from these.*

Keywords: bilingualism; code-switching; codemeshing; Dynamic Systems Theory; linguistic creativity; multimodalities; translanguaging; translanguaging instinct; translingual practices

García, Ofelia, and Li Wei. *Translanguaging: Language, Bilingualism and Education.* Basingstoke: Palgrave Macmillan, 2014. DOI: 10.1057/9781137385765.

The development of a translanguaging theory

The term *translanguaging* comes from the Welsh *trawsieithu* and was coined by Cen Williams (1994, 1996). In its original use, it referred to a pedagogical practice where students are asked to alternate languages for the purposes of receptive or productive use; for example, students might be asked to read in English and write in Welsh and vice versa (Baker, 2011). Since then, the term has been extended by many scholars (for example, Blackledge and Creese, 2010; Canagarajah, 2011a, 2011b; Creese and Blackledge, 2010; García, 2009a, 2011c, 2014b; García and Sylvan, 2011; Hornberger and Link, 2012; Lewis, Jones and Baker, 2012a, 2012b; Li Wei, 2011b; Lin, forthcoming; Sayer, 2012) to refer to both the complex language practices of plurilingual individuals and communities, as well as the pedagogical approaches that use those complex practices (more on the pedagogical approach in Part II of this book). Each of these scholars, however, defines translanguaging slightly differently. And yet, as the discussion of how these scholars treat 'translanguaging' will show, the concept of translanguaging is based on radically different notions of language and bilingualism than those espoused in the 20th century, an epistemological change that is the product of acting and languaging in our highly technological globalized world. We start by tracing the development of the term translanguaging in its relationship to language and bilingualism.

Working within the Welsh tradition, Baker, who first translated the Welsh term as 'translanguaging', defines it as 'the process of making meaning, shaping experiences, gaining understanding and knowledge through the use of two languages' (2011: 288). Lewis, Jones and Baker further claim that in translanguaging,

> both languages are used in a dynamic and functionally integrated manner to organise and mediate mental processes in understanding, speaking, literacy, and, not least, learning. Translanguaging concerns effective communication, function rather than form, cognitive activity, as well as language production. (2012a: 1)

Both these definitions go beyond additive concepts of bilingualism, but yet refer to two languages.

Translanguaging, for us, goes beyond the concept of the two languages of additive bilingualism or interdependence, as we described in our discussion of Figure 1.1, but also of languaging previously discussed. For us, the

DOI: 10.1057/9781137385765

trans- prefix relates to the concept of *transculturación* coined in the 1940s by the Cuban anthropologist Fernando Ortiz. In the prologue to Ortiz's monumental study *Contrapunteo cubano del tabaco y del azúcar* (1940/1978), Bronislaw Malinowski explains that *transculturación* refers to:

> A process in which *a new reality emerges,* compounded and complex; a reality that is not a mechanical agglomeration of characters, not even a mosaic, but a new phenomenon, original and independent. (4, García's translation and italics)

In the same way, for us translanguaging does not refer to two separate languages nor to a synthesis of different language practices or to a hybrid mixture. Rather translanguaging refers to *new* language practices that make visible the complexity of language exchanges among people with different histories, and releases histories and understandings that had been buried within fixed language identities constrained by nation-states (see Mignolo, 2000). Interestingly enough, the title of Ortiz's book refers to a *contrapunteo*. In music a 'counterpoint' is the relationship between musical lines that sound different, move independently and have different motifs, but that sound harmonious when played simultaneously and against each other, an element prevalent in the music of Johann Sebastian Bach. Translanguaging is the enaction of language practices that use different features that had previously moved independently constrained by different histories, but that now are experienced against each other in speakers' interactions as one *new* whole. As such, translanguaging also has much to do with Derrida's concept of *brissure*; that is, practices where difference and sameness occur in an apparently impossible simultaneity.

Canagarajah (2011a) provides us with a definition of translanguaging as 'the ability of multilingual speakers to shuttle between languages, treating the diverse languages that form their repertoire as an *integrated* system' (401, our emphasis). We agree with most of this definition. Canagarajah then argues that this translanguaging ability is part of the *multicompetence* of bilingual speakers (Cook, 2008) whose lives, minds and actions are necessarily different from monolingual speakers because two languages co-exist in their minds, and their complex interactions are always in the foreground (Franceschini, 2011). Multicompetence regards the languages of a multilingual individual as an inter-connected whole – an eco-system of mutual interdependence. From this perspective, the idea of a single language as a reducible set of abstract structures

DOI: 10.1057/9781137385765

or as a mental entity is effectively misleading. And yet, our concept of translanguaging, as we will see in what follows, goes beyond the idea of the multicompetence of bilingual speakers.

Translanguaging and code-switching

Translanguaging differs from the notion of code-switching in that it refers not simply to a shift or a shuttle between two languages, but to the speakers' construction and use of original and complex interrelated discursive practices that cannot be easily assigned to one or another traditional definition of a language, but that make up the speakers' complete language repertoire. Translanguaging, García (2009a) posits is:

> an approach to bilingualism that is centered not on languages as has been often the case, but on the practices of bilinguals that are readily observable. These worldwide translanguaging practices are seen here not as marked or unusual, but rather taken for what they are, namely the normal mode of communication that, with some exceptions in some monolingual enclaves, characterizes communities throughout the world. (44)

García (2009a) continues, 'translanguaging are *multiple discursive practices* in which bilinguals engage in order to *make sense of their bilingual worlds*' (45, emphasis in original). A translanguaging lens posits that 'bilinguals have *one linguistic repertoire* from which they select features *strategically* to communicate effectively. That is, translanguaging takes as its starting point the *language practices of bilingual people as the norm*, and not the language of monolinguals, as described by traditional usage books and grammars' (García, 2012: 1, emphasis in original). Likewise, Blackledge and Creese (2010) speak about flexible bilingualism 'without clear boundaries, which places the speaker at the heart of the interaction' (109).

An illustration that García has used in many lectures about the epistemological difference between code-switching and translanguaging has to do with the language function on the iPhone. The language-switch function could be said to respond to a code-switching epistemology where bilinguals are expected to 'switch' languages. But especially in texting, bilinguals' language practices are not constrained by outside societal forces; and thus features of their entire semiotic repertoire may be selected. Some of these features are visual – emoticons and photographs; other features are textual, defined societally as different 'languages'. For bilinguals, able to use their semiotic repertoire without constraints

DOI: 10.1057/9781137385765

in texting, the language-switch function of the iPhone is useless. For García, then, a translanguaging epistemology would be like turning off the language-switch function on the iPhone and enabling bilinguals to select features from their entire semiotic repertoire, and not solely from an inventory that is constrained by societal definitions of what is an appropriate 'language'.

Translanguaging as bilingual norm

Translanguaging is the discursive norm in bilingual families and communities. For example, the only way to communicate in bilingual/multilingual family events is to translanguage. There are always family members who have different language practices, and thus to communicate with them, speakers have to select certain features of their multilingual repertoire, while excluding others. And there are always events and topics for which certain features in the multilingual repertoire are more relevant than others (Lanza, 2007). A bilingual family conversation about school, for example, might take place with speakers selecting features associated with the language that is dominant in society; whereas the same speakers, when conversing about intimate relationships might select very different features. Other times, talk in family is translanguaged precisely because it signals fluid language practices, now often released, in the family intimacy, from the social external conventions that tie them to one or another 'language'.

Likewise, signage in bilingual communities is often translanguaged. Sometimes this is so because the makers of the sign want to ensure that it appeals to speakers who use various language practices or because the message that it wants to convey to distinctive speakers is indeed different. But most times those who design translanguaged signs understand that bilingual speakers have one linguistic repertoire and that capturing features from socially constructed different languages is more appealing to bilingual speakers. For example, when the beer industry wants to ensure that US Latinos drink a certain brand of beer, a translanguaged advertisement that says: 'A Nuevo Twist on Refreshment', works much better than one conceived in Spanish only or in English only. The translanguaged advertisement reflects also the type of beer, inspired by a Mexican recipe with lime and salt. Translanguaging captures not only the message for bilingual Latinos, but also their cultural hybridity. The act of translanguaging constructs a social space for bilingual individuals

DOI: 10.1057/9781137385765

within families and communities that enables them to bring together all their language and cultural practices. The significance of this translanguaging space is the subject of the next section.

A translanguaging space

Li Wei (2011b) refers to a *translanguaging space* where the interaction of multilingual individuals 'breaks down the artificial dichotomies between the macro and the micro, the societal and the individual, and the social and the psycho in studies of bilingualism and multilingualism' (1234). A translanguaging space allows multilingual individuals to integrate social spaces (and thus 'language codes') that have been formerly practiced separately in different places. For Li Wei (2011b), translanguaging is going both *between* different linguistic structures, systems and modalities, and going *beyond* them. He claims that the act of translanguaging:

> creates a social space for the multilingual user by bringing together different dimensions of their personal history, experience and environment, their attitude, belief and ideology, their cognitive and physical capacity into one coordinated and meaningful performance. (1223)

Li Wei explains that a translanguaging space has its own transformative power because it is forever ongoing and combines and generates new identities, values and practices. Translanguaging, according to Li Wei, embraces both *creativity*; that is, following or flouting norms of language use, as well as *criticality*; that is, using evidence to question, problematize or express views (Li Wei, 2011a, 2011b). Multilingualism by the very nature of the phenomenon is a rich source of creativity and criticality, as it entails tension, conflict, competition, difference and change in a number of spheres, ranging from ideologies, policies and practices to historical and current contexts (Li Wei and Martin, 2009). Enhanced contacts between people of diverse backgrounds and traditions provide new opportunities for innovation and creativity. Individuals are capable of responding to historical and present conditions critically. Speakers consciously construct and constantly modify their sociocultural identities and values through social practices such as translanguaging.

Translanguaging goes beyond hybridity theory that recognizes the complexity of people's everyday spaces and multiple resources to make sense of the world (Bhabha, 1994; Gutiérrez, Baquedano-López and

DOI: 10.1057/9781137385765

Tejeda, 1999). A translanguaging space has much to do with the vision of Thirdspace (one word) articulated by Soja (1996) as:

> a space of extraordinary openness, a place of critical exchange where the geographical imagination can be expanded to encompass a multiplicity of perspectives that have heretofore been considered by the epistemological referees to be incompatible, uncombinable. It is a space where issues of race, class, and gender can be addressed simultaneously without privileging one over the other; where one can be Marxist and post-Marxist, materialist and idealist, structuralist and humanist, disciplined and transdisciplinary at the same time. (5)

Soja critiques binaries, and proposes that it is possible to generate new knowledges and new discourses in a Thirdspace. To frame his Thirdspace, Soja uses the Argentinean Jorge Luis Borges' short story, 'El Aleph,' of which Borges (1971) says it is 'where all places are seen from every angle, each standing clear, without any confusion or blending'; that is, 'the sum total of the spatial universe' (189). A translanguaging space acts as a Thirdspace which does not merely encompass a mixture or hybridity of first and second languages; instead it invigorates languaging with new possibilities from a site of 'creativity and power,' as bell hooks (1990: 152) says. Going *beyond* language refers to transforming the present, to intervening by reinscribing our human, historical commonality in the act of languaging.

Translanguaging and Dynamic Systems Theory

From a Dynamic Systems Theory perspective, translanguaging is a creative process that is the property of the agents' way of acting in interactions, rather than belonging to the language system itself (Shanker and King, 2002: 206; see also De Bot, Lowie and Verspoor, 2007). Translanguaging, for us, is rooted on the principle that bilingual speakers 'soft assemble' their various language practices in ways that fit their communicative situations (García, 2009c, 2014b). That is, bilinguals call upon different social *features* in a seamless and complex network of multiple semiotic signs, as they adapt their languaging to suit the immediate task. Translanguaging, as a soft-assembled mechanism, emerges with enaction, with each action being locally and uniquely situated to satisfy contextual constraints, and creating an interdependence among all components of the system (Kloss and Van Orden, 2009; Turvey and Carello, 1981). Although all speakers have always been engaged in translanguaging, it will be even more

DOI: 10.1057/9781137385765

important in a future of virtual interactions when we would need to engage in fluid language practices and to soft-assemble features that can 'travel' across geographic spaces to enable us to participate, as well as to resist, our more globalized world.

Translanguaging is not limited to oral interactions, but has always encompassed other modalities. The next section explores translanguaging in writing, a most important modality in the world today.

Translanguaging and writing

In contemporary society, writing in a dominant language is seen as 'the sine qua non condition for education and culture' (Menezes de Souza, 2007: 155), although this is not so in all spaces and has not been this way for all times. Because of the interest in writing as a technology or code for dominant languages and not as a series of ideological social practices (Street, 1993), the study of *written multilingual discourse* has been under-researched (Sebba, 2012). But translanguaging in writing has been common from ancient times to today. J. N. Adams (2003: xx–xxi) reminds us, speaking about code-switching, that 'There is a mass of evidence for the practice from Roman antiquity, in primary sources (inscriptions and papyri) and literature (e.g. Plautus, Lucilius and Cicero), and involving several languages in addition to Greek in contact with Latin.' Bilingual texts, as well as transliterated texts where, for example, Latin inscriptions and texts were written in Greek characters, and Greek texts were written in Latin script, abound from the early Roman Republic to the late Empire in the 4th century (Adams, 2003: 40–67). But also prevalent in Classical times were 'mixed-language texts' where the writer used different language conventions and scripts. Adams (2003: 69) says: 'Cicero probably used Greek script in his letters when he switched to Greek.' And there is much evidence of how script and spellings typical of one language were used in writing another.

Writers translanguage to make sense of themselves and their audience. Some languages, such as Wolof, Pular and Manyika, are written in either Arabic or Roman scripts or a combination of the two, depending on writers and audience (Makoni, Makoni, Abdelhay and Mashiri, 2012). Bilingual literary writers often write in one or another language (see, for example, Joseph Conrad who was born in Ukraine to Polish parents but wrote mostly in English, or Eva Hoffman who moved to Canada from Poland at the age of 13, but uses English). As more and

DOI: 10.1057/9781137385765

more bilingual authors are published, many self-translate themselves into one or another language. This is, for example, the case of the Puerto Rican novelist Rosario Ferré who first wrote her novels in Spanish and self-translated them into English, and then wrote one in English and self-translated it into Spanish. What is called 'mixed-language' bilingual writing is also becoming more prevalent today. For example, in the US, Spanish/English bilinguals, writing in English, are using translanguaging strategically for literary effect. This is the case, for example, of the writing of the Dominican-American Junot Díaz, the 2008 Pulitzer winner for his novel, *The Brief Wondrous Life of Oscar Wao* (2007). In the novel, Spanish 'interjects' into an English sentence often; for example, when Beli confronts the Gangster's wife, and says: 'Cómeme el culo, you ugly disgusting vieja' (141). Junot Díaz explains what he calls his 'mash-up of codes' which also includes no quotes, no italics, no way to privilege one or another way of speaking:

> By keeping the Spanish as normative in a predominantly English text, I wanted to remind readers of the fluidity of languages, the mutability of languages. And to mark how steadily English is transforming Spanish and Spanish is transforming English. (Díaz cited in Ch'ien, 2005: 204)

And in a 2013 interview, Díaz adds:

> I think I have no more understanding of the way the immense wave of language works than a guy that surfs really well and speaks to this profound understanding of oceanic forces. The older I get and the more time I spend in language work, the more aware I am of how little I understand the powerful forces that have allowed both English and Spanish to spread across the world, to thrive, to create entirely *new* edifices for themselves, which permits the kind of *linguistic simultaneity* that I so thrill in. (our emphasis, n.p.)

Today new technologies have enabled the production of more fluid language texts (Sebba, 2012; Sebba, Mahootian and Jonsson, 2011). Digital genres such as e-mails (Hinrichs, 2006), online discussion forums, blogging (Montes-Alcalá, 2007) and instant messaging (Lam, 2009) have brought translanguaging in multimodal writing to the forefront. Likewise, the marketization that has accompanied globalization has spurred translanguaging in advertisements as a way to address a public with a bilingual, rather than a monolingual identity. The work on linguistic landscapes has especially made evident the use of translanguaging in written signs, especially in urban landscapes (see Gorter, 2006; Shohamy, Ben Rafael and Barni, 2010; Shohamy and Gorter, 2009). Makoni and

DOI: 10.1057/9781137385765

Makoni (2010) examine, for example, the combination of what they call 'plurilanguaging' and multimodality within the lingual culture of taxis in Ghana and South Africa. The next section focuses on the intersections of translanguaging with multimodalities and social semiotics.

Translanguaging and multimodalities

Our notion of translanguaging foregrounds the different ways multilingual speakers employ, create and interpret different kinds of linguistic signs to communicate across contexts and participants and perform their different subjectivities. Bailey points out that there are tensions and conflicts among different signs because of the sociohistorical associations they carry with them (2007: 257). The focus on signs in our conceptualization of translanguaging enables us to investigate the multimodal nature of communication, especially obvious in complex multilingual contexts.

Successful multilingual interactions have always been aided by multimodalities – gestures, objects, visual cues, touch, tone, sounds and other modes of communication besides words (Khubchandani, 1997; Norris, 2004). And multimodal texts have always been part of writing, as shown, for example, by Menezes De Souza (2007) for the Kashinawas of Brazil. Enhanced today by advanced technologies, all communication is even more *multimodal* than it has been in the past. Multimodal communication refers to that which is typically done through a mixture of gesture, oral performance, artistic, linguistic, digital, electronic, graphic and artifact-related signs (Pahl and Rowsell, 2006). The theoretical underpinnings of multimodality studies can be traced not only to Linguistics, in particular to Halliday's social semiotic theory of communication (Halliday, 1978), but also to cognitive and sociocultural research (Arnheim, 1969), as well as anthropological and social approaches (Goffman, 1979) (see Jewitt, 2008: 357–358). Bezemer and Kress define a *mode* as 'a socially and culturally shaped resource for making meaning' (image, writing, speech, moving image, action, artifacts) (2008: 6). Kress and van Leeuwen (2001) talk about *multimodal social semiotics*, which focuses on signs in all forms, as well as the sign makers and the social environments in which these signs are produced. They go on to argue that meaning-makers or 'sign makers' can make meaning drawing on a variety of modes that do not occur in isolation but always with others in ensembles. Moreover, different modes may share similar and/or different

DOI: 10.1057/9781137385765

'modal resources'; for example, writing has syntactic, grammatical and graphic resources, whereas image has assets that include the position of elements in a frame, size, color or shape. These differences in resources, they further argue, have important implications for the ways modes can be used to accomplish different kinds of semiotic work, which means that 'modes have different affordances – potentials and constraints for making meaning' (Kress and van Leeuwen, 2001: 22). Multimodal social semiotics views all linguistic signs as part of a wider repertoire of modal resources that sign makers have at their disposal and that carry particular sociohistorical and political associations. In a social semiotic approach, language is central to other modes that sign makers can choose from for meaning-making and social identification. Translanguaging for us includes all meaning-making modes.

Translanguaging and transformations

Scollon and Scollon (2004) have proposed that certain actions, such as translanguaging, whether in speech or writing, transform a whole cycle of actions during which each action is transformed. They refer to this phenomenon as *resemiotization*. Actions are resemiotized, that is, they are redesigned, from one semiotic mode to another, with new meanings emerging all the time. Iedema (2003) refers to resemiotization with particular reference to multimodality. He argues that the inevitably transformative dynamics of socially situated meaning-making processes require an additional and alternative analytical point of view. Scollon and Scollon (2004) advocate that the following question be asked: 'Is the action under examination a point at which resemiotization or semiotic transformation occur?' (170). This is what Li Wei (2011b) proposed as 'moment analysis', moving the analytic focus from frequency and regularity to *creative and critical moments* where a specific action leads to a transformation of a cycle of actions. In the next section we consider further this relationship between linguistic creativity and translanguaging, and specifically we question how this impacts the field of Linguistics.

Translanguaging, Linguistics and linguistic creativity

So far we have tried to argue that translanguaging better captures the sociolinguistic realities of everyday life. Does the concept have any value

DOI: 10.1057/9781137385765

for the theoretical field of Linguistics? Since the so-called Chomsky revolution, theoretical linguistics seems to have been rather obsessed with characterizing language as entirely natural, a biological, generic endowment, downplaying, even denying, the diversity of particular languages. In the meantime, however, Chomsky himself, and many of his followers, also seem keen on understanding human beings' capacity to utter an infinite number of sentences based on a finite set of rules of mental grammar and with a finite number of words in their brain. This capacity has been described as 'linguistic creativity' (Chomsky, 1966) which is predetermined by innate forces. Moreover, this innate capacity is believed to enable the novice to acquire different, and sometimes multiple, languages, often in linguistically deprived environments. Pinker popularized these ideas with his book *The Language Instinct* (1994), where he describes language as a discrete combinatorial system, like genes, that has the capacity to generate an infinite number of combinations and permutations out of a finite number of discrete elements. A consequence of the discrete combinatorial system is that human beings not only can interpret ungrammaticality using the fixed code, or Universal Grammar (UG), but also instinctively know when a well-structured string of words do not make sense; yet, they can exploit that fact for the fun of it. Linguistic creativity in the Chomskyan sense is then nothing more than the combination of a finite set of discrete items following a finite set of rules, all of which could be accounted for in UG.

Some psychologists and psycholinguists, while sympathetic to Chomsky's overall goal of making Linguistics a scientific discipline, have argued that Chomskyan linguists pay insufficient attention to experimental data from language processing, with the consequence that Chomskyan theories are not psychologically plausible. In particular, they have challenged the necessity to posit Universal Grammar to explain language acquisition, arguing that domain-general learning mechanisms are sufficient (Elman et al., 1996; Tomasello, 2003, 2008). In the meantime, in their own camp as it were, some have begun to question whether Universal Grammar can in fact be a theory of all languages as Chomsky intended it to be. As mentioned in Chapter 1, Burton-Roberts (2004), for example, argues that since particular languages are social conventions, not biological endowments, Universal Grammar, when conceived as an innate singular, and biologically based language, cannot be used as a generic term for all languages.

DOI: 10.1057/9781137385765

What seems to be at issue is how to understand the creativity of human action, including linguistic creativity. Having the capacity to produce what Pinker describes as the 'sheer vastness of language' using a *fixed* set of rules of action does not necessarily mean a *closed* system. In fact, it may well suggest the opposite, that of an open-ended, complex, adaptive system. Recent research in the cognitive sciences has demonstrated that the processes of human interaction, along with domain-general cognitive processes, shape the structure and knowledge of language. These processes are not independent from one another but are facets of the same *complex adaptive system* (CAS). As the group known as The Five Graces argues (2009: 1–2):

> Language as a CAS involves the following key features: The system consists of multiple agents (the speakers in the speech community) interacting with one another. The system is adaptive, that is, speakers' behaviour is based on their past interactions, and current and past interactions together feed forward into future behaviour. A speaker's behaviour is the consequence of competing factors ranging from perceptual constraints to social motivations. The structures of language emerge from interrelated patterns of experience, social interaction, and cognitive mechanisms.

Applying the Complex Adaptive System approach to language, researchers in language acquisition have explored what they call the Interactional Instinct (Lee et al., 2009), a biologically based drive for human beings to attach, bond and affiliate with others. This instinct leads children to seek out verbal interaction with caregivers and allows them to become competent language speakers. It also explains some of the reasons for the successes and failures in the acquisition of an additional language, in literacy development, and in language use in schizophrenia (see studies in Joaquin and Schumann, 2013). From this perspective, language is not acquired as a result of a Language Acquisition Device in the brain, but is rather a cultural artifact universally acquired by all typical children. Moreover, the Interactional Instinct is at the root of human sociality (Enfield and Levinson, 2006); it is what makes us not only human, but effective social actors in everyday life.

While we also see language as a complex adaptive system, we emphasize, in our notion of translanguaging, the interconnectedness between the traditionally and conventionally understood languages and other human communicative systems. In our view, human beings' knowledge of language cannot be separated from their knowledge of human

DOI: 10.1057/9781137385765

relations and human social interaction, which includes the history, the context of usage and the emotional and symbolic values of specific socially constructed languages. We see translanguaging as having the capacity to broaden the scope of contemporary Linguistics, to look at linguistic realities of the world today and how human beings use their linguistic knowledge holistically to function as language users and social actors. Linguistic creativity therefore needs to be reinterpreted as the language user's ability to play with various linguistic features as well as the various spatial and temporal resonances of these features. Kramsch and Whiteside (2008) have called this ability *symbolic competence,* 'the ability not only to approximate or appropriate for oneself someone else's language, but to shape the very context in which the language is learned and used' (664), hence the transformative capacity of translanguaging. Translanguaging enables the creativity that Li Wei (2011b) has defined as 'the ability to choose between following and flouting the rules and norms of behaviour, including the use of language, and to push and break boundaries between the old and the new, the conventional and the original, and the acceptable and the challenging' (94).

Linguistic creativity and the Translanguaging Instinct

Everyday communication involves traditional linguistic signs (letters) and images, emoticons and pictures. Nicholas and Starks (2014) use the heart image that has become an iconic element in expressions of affection for particular cities, for example, 'I ♥ NY', to illustrate the interconnectedness of all signs. It is also an example of translanguaging, where an image of a heart (traditionally understood as a noun) is used in the linguistic construction in the place that is usually occupied by a verb. Yet when the expression is 'read out', most people would say 'I love New York' rather than 'I heart New York', so changing the grammatical status of the 'word' to which the image is linked. As Nicholas and Starks argue, 'examples such as these reinforce the variation and creativity of speakers as they bring together multiple elements of rich and complex communicative resources.' Research evidence shows that children, even infants, have no problem using their multiple semiotic resources to interpret different forms of symbolic references (Namy and Waxman, 1998; Plester et al., 2011). Human beings have a natural Translanguaging Instinct.

DOI: 10.1057/9781137385765

Let us see some other examples that expand upon the now familiar translanguaging sign of I ♥ X. Figure 2.1 may look like a fairly simple, bilingual extension of I ♥ X, with the word 'China' written out in Chinese characters. Yet, in the original design, reproduced here in black and white, the colors are purposefully chosen. The words and the heart image are yellow, printed on a red T-shirt. This is because the Chinese national flag is red, with five yellow stars – one big one and four smaller ones – in the corner. Figure 2.2, which is frequently found on various merchandise in China, is more abstract and more complex. Instead of

FIGURE 2.1   *I love China a*

FIGURE 2.2   *I love China b*

DOI: 10.1057/9781137385765

the word China written out, the heart image is reinscribed in red with five yellow stars at one corner, exactly the same as in the design of the Chinese national flag. The process of creating these signs, and the process of interpreting them, is a process of translanguaging, involving words, images, symbols and colors, all of which are culturally and historically specific and significant. Understanding the meaning of signs like these require the understanding of not only the linguistic structure but also all the other indexical cues that together make up the signs.

An extension of these translanguaging signs is Figure 2.3 where the heart symbol is replaced by an image of a shamrock, and Obama's name is spelled in a mock Irish fashion. When we asked a random selection of people how they would 'read' the sign, they said either 'I love Obama' or 'Ireland loves Obama'. The shamrock image is reinscribed with the meaning that is conventionally symbolized by the heart symbol to mean 'love'.

FIGURE 2.3   *Shamrock and Obama*

Another example of creative translanguaging that involves perhaps even more complex processes of resemiotization and reinscription is the ObaMao image, purportedly created by a Chinese self-made entrepreneur named Liu Mingjie, who superimposed Barack Obama's face in Chairman Mao's Red Army uniform, in the Chinese revolution woodprint style. The design is now used in a variety of tourist souvenirs, adding some 'Chinglish' phrases – funny, direct English translations of Chinese phrases – and 'Serve the people' in Mao's calligraphy, as Figure 2.4 shows.

DOI: 10.1057/9781137385765

I give you some color to see see

FIGURE 2.4 *ObaMao image*

The Chinglish phrase is a direct translation from the Chinese expression 给你点颜色看看, meaning 'I'll show you some color' or 'I'll teach you a lesson.' This is set in direct contrast with Mao's slogan 'Serve the people'. When the design was first shown on the Internet, there were comments from online bloggers that the expression could be misinterpreted as slightly racist, referring to Obama being black. But the image could be widely seen in Beijing when the US President visited China in 2009, and did not receive any negative reaction in the United States. Yet, the fact that the design, with the linguistic expressions on it, is open to different interpretations is precisely the point of translanguaging that we wish to highlight. When Linguistics focuses narrowly on language as a discrete system of a fixed set of rules, none of the intricacies of

DOI: 10.1057/9781137385765

human creativity, human interaction and human knowledge can be fully understood. Taking a translanguaging approach to the discipline of Linguistics can help to make it more open, democratic and socially relevant. Moreover, the translanguaging perspective provides deeper insights into not only how human beings think, but also why they think the way they do.

In the next section we review other terms that are being used to capture the complexity of interactions in the 21st century. We discuss these terms and draw distinctions between our theory of translanguaging as we have defined it earlier, and these new emerging terms.

Translanguaging and related terms

The shift in the literature on bilingualism/multilingualism from a description of languages as different systems of structures to one emphasizing the fluid language practices of speakers has recently produced a plethora of terms to capture this new linguistic reality (see May, 2013). The Bakhtinian concept of *heteroglossia*, referred to earlier, serves as an umbrella term for all of these practices, including that of translanguaging. As Bailey (2007) has shown, taking up heteroglossia for analysis focuses attention on alternations of officially authorized codes, without neglecting 'the diversity of socially indexical linguistic features within codes' (268). Bailey argues:

> Heteroglossia can encompass socially meaningful forms in both bilingual and monolingual talk; it can account for the multiple meanings and readings of forms that are possible, depending on one's subject position; and it can connect historical power hierarchies to the meanings and valences of particular forms in the here-and-now. (267)

We discuss later a number of alternative terms being used, all pointing to the fluidity of language practices in the world today – crossing, transidiomatic practices, polylingualism, metrolingualism, multivocality, codemeshing, bilanguaging and the 'glish' terms such as Spanglish, Singlish, etc. We argue, however, that for us the term translanguaging is better able to capture the trans-systemic and transformative practices as a new language reality emerges. In addition, our concept of translanguaging resists the danger that Flores (2013) has warned against in the blind acceptance of plurilingualism. Flores

DOI: 10.1057/9781137385765

(2013) cautions that in adopting a translanguaging stance we might simply be preparing flexible workers to advance the neoliberal agenda. Translanguaging for us, however, is part of a moral and political act that links the production of alternative meanings to transformative social action. As such, translanguaging contributes to the social justice agenda. This in itself distinguishes our concept from many others that we discuss here.

Crossing

We start with Ben Rampton's notion of *crossing*, which refers to the use of language practices of out-group members for purposes of temporary identity representation and to resist the authority of their teachers. In his pioneering study of a multiethnic secondary school in inner London, Rampton (1995) showed how and when different language varieties were integrated into ordinary talk.

Rampton's concept of crossing is related to *stylization*, defined by Bakhtin (1981) as a performance in which speakers produce an artistic image of another's language. Although Rampton's notion of crossing has been very influential in disrupting the direct link between language and identity that had been constructed since the 19th-century work of the German Romantics, crossing seems to connote going from one autonomous language to another, a concept that our definition of translanguaging would challenge.

Transidiomatic practice

Jacquemet (2005) coins the term *transidiomatic practices* to refer to the 'communicative practices of transnational groups that interact using different languages and communicative codes, simultaneously present in a range of communicative channels, both local and distant' (264–265). Jacquemet adds: 'Transidiomatic practices are the results of the co-presence of multilingual talk (exercised by de/reterritorialized speakers) and electronic media, in contexts heavily structured by social indexicalities and semiotic codes' (265). Jacquemet's work, focused on communication in the Adriatic region, highlights the complex connectivity and flow of global processes and diasporic social formations. He reminds us that language contact between groups is not new, although the 'extraordinary simultaneity and co-presence of the languages' (271) is

DOI: 10.1057/9781137385765

novel. He then calls for a 'linguistics of *xenoglossic becoming,* transidiomatic mixing, and communicative recombinations' (274, emphasis added). Although Jacquemet's work makes evident that the deterritorialization of communicative practices brought about through diasporic social formations, media and global power elites does construct new transidiomatic practices, neither the concept of language itself, nor the power dynamics involved in these constructions, are questioned. Jacquemet problematizes traditional sociolinguistic conceptions of language, but does not challenge the existence of language as a system of structures that is merely recombined.

Polylingualism

In contrast, Jørgensen (2008) argues that it doesn't make sense to talk of 'a language' per se, although he defends the concept of 'language'. He agrees with Makoni and Pennycook (2007) and Heller (2010) that languages are constructs that cannot be counted or categorized. And he claims that language in itself consists of human behavior between people by which we form and shape our social structures. He convincingly argues:

> The concept of *a* language is thus bound in time and space…, and it is not part of our understanding of the human concept of language. Features are, however. Speakers use features and not languages. Features may be ascribed to specific languages (or specific categories which are called languages). This may be an important quality of a feature, and one which speakers may know and use as they speak. But what the speaker uses is a feature. (166, our emphasis)

In referring to language use, especially by young people in urban late modern societies that simultaneously use features from different sets, Jørgensen (2008) and Møller (2008) use the term *polylingualism.* The term refers to the combination of features that are not discrete and complete 'languages' in themselves but that are bound up in change. Jørgensen distinguishes polylingualism from multilingualism because polylingual behavior is a combination of features that are used side-by-side, whereas multilingualism refers to a combination of languages that should be separated. In this aspect, and in arguing for feature-based languaging, polylingualism comes close to our concept of translanguaging.

DOI: 10.1057/9781137385765

Metrolingualism

Otsuji and Pennycook (2010) refer to fluid practices in urban contexts as *metrolingualism,* as in translanguaging rejecting the notion that there are discrete languages or codes. They argue:

> Metrolingualism describes the ways in which people of different and mixed backgrounds use, play with and negotiate identities through language; it does not assume connections between language, culture, ethnicity, nationality or geography, but rather seeks to explore how such relations are produced, resisted, defied or rearranged. Its focus is *not on language systems* but on languages as emergent from contexts of interaction. (246, emphasis added)

Otsjui and Pennycook (2010, 2011) focus on a metrolingual space where people 'undo, queer and reconstitute their linguistic practices between the orthodox and heterodox' (424). Metrolingualism focuses on social practices that are in a state of construction and disarray within urban contexts, and thus, does not go far enough in extending these practices to all contexts, as translanguaging does.

Multivocality

Another term related to translanguaging is that of *multivocality,* proposed by Higgins (2009) in her study of language practices in Kenya and Tanzania. Based on Bakhtin's concept of voice, multivocality for Higgins refers to the idea that multilingual utterances, because of their syncretic nature, convey all possible meanings simultaneously because they are, as Woolard (1998) suggests, *bivalent.* That is, by belonging to two languages at once and thus allowing double-voiced usages, multilingual utterances allow speakers to 'remain in the interstices of multivocality' (Higgins, 2009, 7).

Multivocality has in common with translanguaging the multiplicities of meanings of multilingual utterances. However, Higgins considers these multiplicities as organized on the basis of domains or specific activities. Translanguaging goes beyond the sociolinguistic conception of space or domain which orders the multivocality. As Li Wei points out, the act of translanguaging itself creates the social space within the multilingual user that makes it possible to go between different linguistic structures and beyond them. It is *the speakers*, not the space, who are in control of the languaging performance, by bringing

DOI: 10.1057/9781137385765

together 'different dimensions of their personal history, experience and environment, their attitude, belief and ideology, their cognitive and physical capacity' (Li Wei, 2011b: 1223).

Codemeshing and translingual practices

Canagarajah (2011a) reserves the term *codemeshing* to refer to the shuttle between repertoires, especially in writing, for rhetorical effectiveness. He defines codemeshing as 'a communicative device used for specific rhetorical and ideological purposes in which a multilingual speaker intentionally integrates local and academic discourse as a form of resistance, reappropriation and/or transformation of the academic discourse' (Michael-Luna and Canagarajah, 2007: 56). For Canagarajah, codemeshing differs from codeswitching in that it refers to one single integrated system. Like translanguaging, codemeshing signals one single integrated system, but whereas codemeshing is seen as a form of resistance, translanguaging is positioned as the discursive norm that names a reality other than a monolingual one.

Recently Canagarajah (2013) has coined an all-encompassing term – *translingual practice* – meant to serve as an umbrella for all these dynamic terms surrounding the language practices in multilingual encounters:

> The term translingual conceives of language relationships in more dynamic terms. The semiotic resources in one's repertoire or in society interact more closely, become part of an integrated resource, and enhance each other. The languages mesh in transformative ways, generating new meanings and grammars. (8)

Canagarajah's rejection of the term translanguaging and adoption of translingual practices is based on his claim that translanguaging has been defined in cognitive terms, as a cognitive multicompetence. However, as we have seen in this chapter, what makes translanguaging an important theoretical advance is that it is transdisciplinary; that is, it refers to a meaning-making social *and* cognitive activity that works in-between conventional meaning-making practices and disciplines and goes beyond them, for it emerges from the contextual affordances in the complex interactions of multilinguals. Canagarajah also claims that in codemeshing there is a mixing of communicative modes and diverse symbol systems other than language and that this distinguishes it from translanguaging. For us, however, as we said before all translanguaging is multimodal.

DOI: 10.1057/9781137385765

Bilanguaging

Taking up and extending A. L. Becker's concept of languaging described in Chapter 1, the Argentinean semiotician, Walter Mignolo (2000) uses the term *bilanguaging* to refer not only to the language fluidity of interactions, but also to political action. Mignolo says that the focus of bilanguaging is on 'redressing the asymmetry of languages and denouncing the coloniality of power and knowledge' (231). By bringing the coloniality of power to the foreground and thinking from that colonial difference, Mignolo's bilanguaging calls forth a political process of social transformation. Mignolo's 'bilanguaging love' is offered as a way to correct the violence of systems of control and oppression that colonial expansion and nation building have installed within traditional understandings of language and sign systems.

Translanguaging shares much with Mignolo's concept of bilanguaging. Bilanguaging, like translanguaging, confronts colonial language practices with subaltern ones in a border space; but translanguaging goes beyond a physical space that brings together two realities, as it focuses on the dynamism of the actual complex interaction of speakers with multiple semiotic resources.

Spanglish, Singlish

Monolingual communities and the elite often refer to the fluid ways in which non-dominant communities speak with terms that are stigmatized such as *Spanglish* or *Singlish*. It is interesting that both these terms refer to stigmatized ways of speaking, although they signal different social languages. Singlish refers to what is socially constructed as the colloquial English spoken in Singapore, described as neither Mandarin Chinese nor Standard English (Rubdy, 2005). Despite official visions of Singlish as corrupted English, it is said that 70 per cent of Singaporeans accept it as a mark of solidarity and the symbol of 'Singaporeanness' (Rubdy, 2005). In contrast, Spanglish refers not to what is socially considered English, but to 'corrupted' forms of Spanish used by US Latinos, 'a bastard jargon: part Spanish and part English' (Stavans, 2000: 7; Stavans, 2003). Some Latino scholars claim the term as a badge of bicultural identity (Rosa, 2010; Zentella, 1997, 2008). Otheguy and Stern (2010), however, warn against the use of the term, for it disparages ways of speaking of Latinos, focusing on what is seen as structural

DOI: 10.1057/9781137385765

mixing and unusual hybridity, and separating US Spanish-speakers from others who speak other varieties of popular Spanish throughout the Spanish-speaking world, and marginalizing them.

The appropriation of these terms by ethnolinguistic communities points to the growing fluidity in bilingual speech. But these terms take as their point of departure a 'standard' language, comparing bilingual speech to each of the 'languages', as defined and described by the dominant members of society. In contrast, translanguaging assumes one linguistic repertoire that could never be split into one or another language, an Aleph in the Borgean sense that contains the sum total of the meaning-making universe of bilingual speakers.

Translanguaging is related in different ways to the terms above, and owes a great deal to some of these theoreticians. Yet, as we discussed before, our theory of translanguaging differs in ways that we summarize in the next section.

Translanguaging: a summary and our positionalities

Translanguaging, as we have said, liberates language from structuralist-only or mentalist-only or even social-only definitions. Instead, it signals a trans-semiotic system with many meaning-making signs, primarily linguistic ones that combine to make up a person's semiotic repertoire. Languages then are not autonomous and closed linguistic and semiotic systems. Bilingual speakers select meaning-making features and freely combine them to potentialize meaning-making, cognitive engagement, creativity and criticality. Translanguaging refers to the act of languaging between systems that have been described as separate, and beyond them. As such, translanguaging is transformative and creates changes in inter-active cognitive and social structures that in turn affect our continuous languaging becoming. Finally, in its transdisciplinarity, translanguaging enables us as speakers to go beyond traditional academic disciplines and conventional structures, in order to gain new understandings of human relations and generate more just social structures, capable of liberating the voices of the oppressed.

Translanguaging, as we have seen, offers a transdisciplinary lens that combines sociolinguistic and psycholinguistic perspectives to study the complex multimodal practices of multilingual interactions as social and

DOI: 10.1057/9781137385765

cognitive acts able to transform not only semiotic systems and speaker subjectivities, but also sociopolitical structures. Translanguaging works by generating trans-systems of semiosis, and creating trans-spaces where new language practices, meaning-making multimodal practices, subjectivities and social structures are dynamically generated in response to the complex interactions of the 21st century.

Our positionalities and translanguaging

Before we conclude this chapter, it may be useful to point out that our consideration of translanguaging emerges from our own positionalities as transnational scholars[1] and from what the Argentinean semiotician Walter Mignolo (2000) has called '*border thinking*' (11); that is, understandings that emerge from experiences and thinking between and beyond languages and modes and their historical relations. Border thinking is related to the Chicana scholar Gloria Anzaldúa's *borderlands theory* – the straddling of worlds, languages and cultures that occurs in her *nepantla,* the Nahuatl word for the land in the middle, the space of transformation. In speaking about her identity, Anzaldúa says: 'Neither eagle nor serpent, but both. And like the ocean, neither animal respects borders' (1987: 84). And of her languaging, she says: 'neither español ni inglés, but both' (1987: 77). 'To survive the Borderlands/you must live *sin fronteras*/be a crossroads', she adds (217). Translanguaging provides this space *sin fronteras* – linguistic ones, nationalist ones, cultural ones. Translanguaging for us refers to languaging actions that enact a political process of social and subjectivity transformation which resist the asymmetries of power that language and other meaning-making codes, associated with one or another nationalist ideology, produce. As García (2014b) has said: 'In translanguaging the speaker is situated in a space where alternative representations and enunciations can be generated because buried histories are released and alternative, conflicting knowledges are produced.' Translanguaging resists the historical and cultural positionings of monolingualism or of additive bilingualism, releasing speakers from having to conform to 'parallel monolingualisms' (Heller, 1999) or to traditional linguistic ways of making meaning.

In Part II of this book we turn to considering how translanguaging has the potential to liberate both monolingual and bilingual education from the structural strictures of the past. In particular, we review the

DOI: 10.1057/9781137385765

structures of bilingual education of the 20th century and describe the control of language practices most often exercised by education systems, as well as the agency of learners in violating these strictures through translanguaging. We argue that bilingual education, in the forms of the past, has done little to destroy the hierarchies among languages and people, to ameliorate the lives of language-minoritized students, or to generate learner subjectivities able to engage in, and value, the translanguaging practices which are the norm in bilingual communities. We suggest that translanguaging can be used in education, and particularly in bilingual education, as a transformative practice in order to provide a trans-space of change and an interdisciplinarity of knowledge and understandings. At the same time, we point to how hard it is to accept translanguaging within educational systems that are instruments of the nation-state and how difficult it becomes for us to speak about translanguaging in the context of schools.

Note

1   García was born in Cuba and has lived in New York City from the age of 11. Li Wei was born in Beijing, China, of Manchu-Chinese parentage, and has lived in the UK since his mid-twenties.

DOI: 10.1057/9781137385765

Part II
Education and
Translanguaging

▶

DOI: 10.1057/9781137385765

3
Language, Bilingualism and Education

Abstract: *As the first chapter in Part II, this chapter turns its attention to education. Focusing on the growing multilingualism in schools, the chapter reviews traditional definitions and types of bilingual education. It frames foreign/ second language education, as well as bilingual education, as ways of enacting parallel monolingualisms, and then reviews ways in which this is resisted in classrooms all over the world. It also presents ways in which educators are promoting flexible languaging in teaching, transgressing the strict structures of dual language bilingual classrooms, as well as going beyond the traditional view of separate languages literacies.*

Keywords: bilingual education; CLIL; dual language education; foreign language education; immersion education; second language education

García, Ofelia, and Li Wei. *Translanguaging: Language, Bilingualism and Education*. Basingstoke: Palgrave Macmillan, 2014. DOI: 10.1057/9781137385765.

DOI: 10.1057/9781137385765

Multilingualism and language in education

Government-sponsored schools around the world, for the most part, continue to provide an education only in the powerful language of the state. And yet, most nations in the world today are multilingual, evident from the fact that there are only 196 countries, but seven billion inhabitants who speak close to what are considered 7,000 languages by *Ethnologue* (Lewis, Jones and Baker, 2013). As the Linguistic Society of America stated in 1995: 'the vast majority of the world's nations are at least bilingual, and most are multilingual, even if one ignores the impact of modern migrations' (n.p.). In the 21st century, international migration has accelerated. It is estimated that in 2005 there were nearly 200 million international migrants around the world – a two-and-a-half-fold increase from 1970 (Sollors, 2009). Clearly the linguistic heterogeneity is great.

This greater movement of people and greater consciousness means that the countries of Europe and North America that in the 20th century were constructed as being monolingual (because their indigenous multilingualism was silenced by repression or massacre) are today recognized for being as highly multilingual as Asia, Africa and the Pacific. In Europe, 56 per cent of those polled in 2006 for a European Commission report were at least bilingual, with 28 per cent claiming trilingualism. Even in the UK, 38 per cent of the population is bilingual (Grosjean, 2012). In the US, where indigenous and immigrant languages have traditionally lost ground, 20 per cent of the population over five years of age, approximately 55 million, spoke a language other than English at home in 2007 (US Census Bureau, 2007). Urban centers have become openly superdiverse (Vertovec, 2007). In London, some 300 different languages are spoken. In New York City 52 per cent of the population over five years of age (3,712,467 people) speak a language other than English at home (US Census Bureau, 2009). And in Sub-Saharan Africa, urban vernaculars are spreading (Makoni, Makoni, Abdelhay and Mashiri, 2012).

But despite (and because of) the multilingual reality of the world, state schools continue to insist on monolingual 'academic standard' practices. Schools are permeated with institutional norms and practices that are complicit with the power structures of dominant societies (Bourdieu, 1991; Bourdieu and Passeron, 1990). Even when states are officially bilingual or when bilingual education systems of education are adopted, it is the constructed 'standard academic language' that is used in school.

DOI: 10.1057/9781137385765

The 'standard' language is codified by a central powerful group, and then policed through schools. These dominant language practices are then tied to academic and economic success (Delpit, 2006; Morrell, 2008). This is the reality even in bilingual education programs, as we will see in the next section, for these are also, with few exceptions, instruments of the nation-state.

Bilingual education

Bilingual education distinguishes itself from other forms of language education in that content and language learning are integrated; that is, two or more 'languages' are used as a medium of instruction (Baker, 2011; Cenoz, 2009; García, 2009a). In this book, as we said before (see note 1, chapter 1) we use the term *bilingual education* as an umbrella term to encompass what is also called trilingual and multilingual education. We do so for two reasons – one having to do with continuity and resistance, the other with transformation and extension. We use bilingual education because of its *continued* link to a sociopolitical agenda that insists on the use of minority students' home language practices to provide more equitable educational opportunity, thus affirming the social justice agenda. In contrast, the current use of trilingual and multilingual education most often refers to the addition of a prestigious language, usually English. In naming the enterprise we're describing as bilingual education, we *resist* the dismissal of 'bilingual education' in countries like the United States where bilingual education has been progressively 'silenced' and affirm its potential to educate both language minoritized, as well as language majority youth.

The concept of bilingual education that we will construct through a translanguaging approach *transforms* and extends our current definition, focusing on complex linguistic interactions in classrooms that cannot be simply enumerated as two, three or more. In choosing to continue to talk about bilingual education, *we emphasize that a translanguaging approach in education is not a substitute for bilingual education programs*, important on their own. Rather, translanguaging in education *transforms and extends* traditional bilingual education programs. The prefix 'bi-' in bilingual remits us to the slang 'bi' for a bisexual person, attracting us beyond language practices that conform to culturally predominant ones and that could be counted and separated into different 'languages'. Thus,

DOI: 10.1057/9781137385765

we use the term bilingual education to both affirm our commitment to the inclusion of multiple language practices for social justice, and to extend its usefulness beyond just the use of different separate 'languages', affirming the *bilanguaging love* that Mignolo (2000) proposed and that we considered in Chapter 2 of Part I.

Types of bilingualism in education and bilingual education

In 1974 Wallace Lambert proposed what became the two classic models of viewing bilingualism in schools during the 20th century – *subtractive bilingualism* and *additive bilingualism*. Subtractive bilingualism was said to be what happens when schools take away the home language of the child who speaks a minoritized language and substitutes it with a majority language. Additive bilingualism, on the other hand, was said to refer to when a 'second' language is added whole to the child's 'first' language. However, these models of bilingualism have proven to be insufficient, given the diversity of learners in classrooms today. Although we describe 'types' or 'models' of bilingualism below, we agree with Baetens Beardsmore (2009) that a 'features approach' to describing bilingual programs might be more accurate. Cenoz (2009) has also proposed that the features of multilingual education can be represented in a model based along four continua – (1) subject taught, (2) language of instruction, (3) teacher and (4) school context.

Subtractive bilingualism is sometimes promoted by what are called *transitional bilingual education* models. These programs temporarily use the child's home language to facilitate the acquisition of a dominant language. Although in most programs of this type language-minoritized students are moved to mainstream programs as they move up in the grades or as they acquire the dominant school language, in some transitional programs this is not so. In some programs it is the emphasis on one language or the other that transitions, as more instruction occurs in the dominant language.

In support of the additive bilingualism of children, different types of bilingual education programs have been developed, especially in the 20th century (García, 2009a). *Maintenance bilingual education* is said to serve only non-dominant students whose parents want them to maintain their home language while developing proficiency in a dominant language. These programs exist when the community has obtained some measure of political respect and often reflect the

DOI: 10.1057/9781137385765

group's cultural values, a strong bicultural identity, and even a sense of self-determination for the group. *Prestigious bilingual education* uses an additive approach in teaching dominant language-majority children through the medium of two languages with power. *Immersion bilingual education* is another additive type of bilingual education where, after a short period of time in which language-majority children are taught in the additional language, the home language is increasingly used until more or less half of the instructional time is devoted to the home language and the other half to the additional language. Educational programs organized by ethnic communities, known by various names – *community language schools* in Australia, *ethnic mother-tongue schools* in the US (Fishman, 1966), *heritage language schools* in Canada (Cummins and Danesi, 1990; Danesi, McLeod and Morris, 1993) and also recently, after the restrictions on bilingual education, in the US (Brinton, Kagan and Bauhaus, 2007) – provide instruction in home languages to language-minoritized children. These programs are mostly after-school or weekend programs (see Blackledge and Creese, 2010; Li Wei, 2006; Li Wei and Wu, 2009, for these kinds of programs in the UK, and the ways in which they're changing). What all these programs, responding to additive conceptions of bilingualism, have in common is that they were developed for a language group who were assumed to be homogeneous – minoritized students in the maintenance and heritage type, and majority students in the prestigious and immersion type of bilingual education.

Today, however, with interactions, as we have said, openly occurring in contact spaces (often virtual ones) between speakers of different origins, experiences, characteristics and histories, bilingual education cannot be simply subtractive or additive, for we have come to finally recognize that there are no homogenous groups using the same language practices (see Brubacker, 2009). García and Kleifgen (2010) have proposed another two types of bilingualism for schools – recursive dynamic bilingualism and dynamic bilingualism. *Recursive dynamic bilingualism* refers to the complex nature of the bilingualism of ethnolinguistic groups who have undergone substantial language shift as they attempt language revitalization. For these groups, like the Māoris in New Zealand, *immersion revitalization bilingual education* programs are organized to move their very different language practices (some speakers having experienced more loss than others) into a bilingual future. *Developmental bilingual education* programs also embody this recursive bilingualism because the

DOI: 10.1057/9781137385765

ethnolinguistic group is not monolingual to start with, but rather has diverse language practices and multiple identities. These programs are usually found in language-minoritized communities that have undergone some degree of language loss, but have not suffered the language shift of those who need immersion revitalization bilingual education programs. In practice, because of the great range of bilingual practices evident among students in immersion revitalization bilingual education programs, as well as in developmental bilingual education programs, its recursive bilingualism can be subsumed under the dynamic bilingualism concept that we develop next.

Dynamic bilingualism, as we said before, refers to the multiple language interactions and other linguistic interrelationships that take place on different scales and spaces among multilingual speakers. Today most bilingual education programs include children who have various language practices and who are from many dominant and non-dominant groups. Bilingual education types known as *dual language, two-way bilingual education, two-way immersion, poly-directional bilingual education, bilingual immersion*, deliberately include students with diverse language practices. Even complementary community language programs (Blackledge and Creese, 2010; Li Wei, 2006; Li Wei and Martin, 2009), what García, Zakharia and Otcu (2013) call *bilingual community education*, are adapting to the greater continuum of bilingual proficiency that students bring, as well as to the growing number of language-majority students who attend programs that were originally conceived as being only for 'ethnic' students. Beyond these programs, some groups and even countries aspire to have their entire population fluent in at least three languages. In these places, *multiple multilingual education* uses three or more languages as media of instruction and in literacy instruction (see Cenoz, 2009, for the Basque example). As in other programs, the students are not assumed to be homogeneous.

Despite the presence of recursive and dynamic bilingualism within the bilingual classrooms of today, pedagogic approaches to bilingualism respond to it as additive; that is, as two or more autonomous language systems that need to be separated. Bilingualism continues to be seen by educational authorities that sponsor bilingual education as a set of 'parallel monolingualisms' (Heller, 1999: 5).

Two things are certain about all the bilingual education programs described above. One, bilingual education program structures usually separate languages, insisting that each language be used in its own

DOI: 10.1057/9781137385765

educational space and time period or with different teachers. Orellana and Reynolds (2008), speaking about bilingual education in the US, say:

> Even in bilingual programs, students typically work either in their home language or in English (with language divisions occurring across subject matter or time of day); they are rarely encouraged to draw from the full repertoire of their linguistic toolkits, much less to use translation or code-switching as part of their meaning-making processes. (62)

Two, as we will see, despite language education policies that strictly separate languages, students and teachers constantly violate this principle (Menken and García, 2010). In fact, students and teachers in all bilingual education programs use complex language practices, and build on complex resources for meaning-making in order to learn and teach; that is, they use what we are calling here *translanguaging*. What this looks like, and the effects that translanguaging, as defined in Part I, has on the structures and practices in education programs, and particularly in bilingual education, is the subject of the rest of this book. We warn readers, however, that translanguaging in school often looks (on the surface) like going from one 'language' to another. This has to do with the schools' emphasis on developing standard language for academic purposes. We have also found it difficult to describe what happens in translanguaging as process because the language that we continue to use reflects the social categories of autonomous languages.

As we will see, a translanguaging approach goes beyond the surface, arguing that from the learners' perspective, what produces language as defined in school is the students' own creative languaging, drawing from their entire linguistic repertoire. Translanguaging in classrooms is an approach to bilingualism that is centered not on the acquisition and development of languages, as has often been the case, but on the practices of bilingual students and their teachers that are readily observable and that are different from our traditional conceptions of autonomous languages. Translanguaging is also an approach that can be followed in all classrooms, whether monolingual or bilingual, and by all teachers, whether monolingual or bilingual, for equitable learning. But before we develop the concept of translanguaging in education in the next chapter, it is important to look at how traditional definitions of language and bilingualism are being contested and resisted in education today.

DOI: 10.1057/9781137385765

Monolingualisms in education

Monolingual education is understood as the use of only the dominant language of society or school in education. Language minorities in most countries in the world continue to be educated only in the dominant language without leveraging their home language practices. In the US, the Structured Immersion English programs that followed the outlawing of bilingual education in California (1998), Arizona (2000) and Massachusetts (2002) used English only. And even in programs that supposedly aim to develop bilingualism, as in the foreign/second language and bilingual education programs considered below, the emphasis is on separating languages.

Foreign and second language education and parallel monolingualisms

'Foreign' or 'second' language education programs have had a long history of *separation* – separation of students by language levels to keep input comprehensible, and of languages in teaching to focus attention on the 'target' or dominant language (Howatt, 1984; Yu, 2001). From this perspective, code-switching between the so-called mother-tongue, 'L1' or 'native' language and the 'foreign' or 'L2' language is often seen as a sign of linguistic and cognitive deficiency.

Throughout the 20th century the teaching of 'foreign' languages favored the 'direct method' in which all teaching was done in the 'target' language and grammar was taught inductively, following the way in which children learn their first language. This was followed in the mid-20th century by the development of the audio-lingual method which was based on behaviorist theory and drilled grammar through repetition, and later the communicative method, focusing on interaction in the 'target' language. All methods advocated against the use of translation and encouraged only the use of the 'target' language which was deemed as 'foreign'. 'Foreign language' study was centered on a nation-state ideology that perceived 'other' languages as alien, external and spoken only overseas. These languages were to be kept as distant as possible from the dominant one of the nation-state.

As the worldwide ethnic revival of the 1960s brought the languages of ethnolinguistic minorities and immigrants to the forefront, 'second language programs' were developed to teach the dominant 'standard

DOI: 10.1057/9781137385765

academic' language to minorities. But as in foreign language education, the emphasis was on keeping the languages separate, 'othering' the languages of those who spoke them within the nation-state. A division was made between the students' first language (L1) and their second language (L2), now the object of attention and learning. Second language learners were seen as just that, never able to compete with 'native speakers.' This 'thickening' of the language identities of 'second language' speakers for whom the dominant language could never be 'first' is related to the myth that there is a 'genetic' ownership of language. Bonfiglio (2010) explains:

> 'our native' language, which is 'our birthright,' is seen as endangered by the presence of an other who is perceived as a biological contaminant and thus a threat to the matrix of nation, ethnicity and language. Such ethnolinguistic prejudice continually lurks behind the apparently innocent kinship metaphors employed to describe the authority of the speaker who acquired the language in question as his or her first language. These are metaphors of nativity and maternality found in the locutions 'native speaker,' mother tongue,' 'native language,' *langue maternelle, locuteur natif, Muttersprache, Muttersprachler, lingua maternal, modersprake,* and so on'. (1)

Thus, 'second language' programs that were developed for language-minoritized students in the 1960s ignored and minimized the use of the students' home languages, and many still do so today. And although Stephen Krashen (1981) was an advocate of bilingual education, his theory that 'acquisition', that is, the subconscious development of a 'second' language, was better than 'learning' it through rule-governed approaches was often used to support English as a Second Language approaches in English only. Second language teachers were led to believe that students were off-task or that their behavior was deviant or disruptive if they were using their home languages (Macaro, 2006).

Bilingual education and parallel monolingualisms

Bilingual programs suffered from the same misconceptions. Immersion bilingual programs in Canada for the Anglophone majority initially used only the child's 'second' language – French. This practice of separating languages in instruction is what Cummins (2007, 2008) has referred to as 'the two solitudes'. This is also the practice in many immersion revitalization programs. For example, in many Māori-controlled schools, Māori is the language of school, except for the 'English building' in which English is used and taught.

DOI: 10.1057/9781137385765

As bilingual programs for language minorities in the US became institutionalized after the Bilingual Education Act (BEA) in 1968, there was an increasing tendency to separate English from the other language. This had to do with the transitional nature of bilingual programs after the first reauthorization of the BEA in 1974. Jacobson and Faltis (1990) explained the reasons for language separation in US bilingual education:

> Bilingual educators have usually insisted on the separation of the two languages, one of which is English and the other, the child's vernacular. By strictly separating the languages, the teacher avoids, it is argued, cross-contamination, thus making it easier for the child to acquire a new linguistic system as he/she internalizes a given lesson. ... (4)

The so-called dual language education or 'dual immersion' model in vogue in the US today continues to insist on separation of the two languages by teacher and/or time of day or subject in order to develop what is seen as parallel developments in the two languages (Lessow-Hurley, 1990; Lindholm-Leary, 2001). Lindholm-Leary (2006: 89) describes dual language programs as having 'periods of instruction during which only one language is used (that is, there is no translation or language mixing).' These separate structures of bilingual education, and the continued use of the terms L1 and L2 reveal an ideology of bilingualism that is *monoglossic* (Del Valle, 2000; García, 2009a). In other words, bilingualism is seen as 'parallel monolingualism' (Heller, 1999).

But despite language policies in bilingual education that insist on separating languages, bilingual students display different language practices. Martínez (2010: 24), for example, reports on this language exchange in an English-Language Arts classroom at a middle school in East Los Angeles in the US:

ZULEMA:	Page what?
CAROLINE:	Um.
ZULEMA:	Twenty-something, no?
Caroline:	Wait. This one? *¿Cómo está?*
ZULEMA:	*Sí*, circle. *¿Cuál es?*
CAROLINE:	*¿Como ésta, mira. Como ésta. Esta está bien bonita.*
ZULEMA:	*Sí, pero ¿qué* page?
CAROLINE:	*A ver, ¿qué* page? Twenty-one.

Because policies and structures of separation have never been enough to keep bilingual use out of instruction, language-minoritized children using home language practices in schools have been, and continue to

DOI: 10.1057/9781137385765

be, severely punished. For example, the Welsh Not, a piece of wood inscribed with the letters WN, was hung around the necks of children who spoke Welsh in schools in Wales in the early 20th century. The last child to wear the 'not' at the end of the school day would be given a beating. In post-colonial contexts, especially in Africa where English or French were supposed to be used exclusively after third or fourth grade, descriptions like this one from Ngugi wa Thing'o (1986), concerning his use of Gikuyi in his Kenyan school, abound:

> The culprit was given corporal punishment – three to five strokes of the cane on bare buttocks – or was made to carry a metal plate around the neck with inscriptions such as I AM STUPID or I AM A DONKEY. Sometimes the culprits were fined with money they could hardly afford. (11)

Today, the punishment is not corporal, but relies on instruction and assessments that follow monolingual language standards, ensuring that bilingual students get lower grades, are made to feel inadequate, and fail in schools.

Annamalai (2005) describes education through the medium of English-only in India thus:

> The teachers, who are not very proficient in English, prepare questions and answers in advance and dictate them to the students, who commit them to memory by copying them many times. There is no classroom interaction in which students express themselves and ask questions on the subjects taught because of 'silencing by English', the way the teacher makes use of the students' inability in English in order to keep them quiet in the class, i.e. by not permitting questions in the students' language. (27)

Silence, memorization and rigid language routines characterize these classrooms. Clearly the educational consequences of the sociopolitical inability to authenticate a multilingual and heteroglossic reality is responsible for educational failure of many language minorities around the world. The following section addresses how teachers and students have often resisted the monoglossic and monolingual ethos of schools.

Beyond monolingualisms in education

Despite the banishment of students' minoritized home languages from many schools and the philosophy of strictly separating languages in

DOI: 10.1057/9781137385765

bilingual education programs, the literature has repeatedly referred to what scholars describe as 'code-switching' as the education norm in the teaching of language-minoritized students, and especially in post-colonial contexts (see, for example, Brock-Utne, 2006, for Tanzania; Bunyi, 2005, for Kenya; Lin, 1999, for Hong Kong; Martin, 2005, for Malaysia; Merritt, 1992, for Kenya; Rubagumya, 1994, for Kenya and Tanzania; Saxena, 2006, for Brunei). Martin (2005) calls code-switching a 'safe' practice because 'a language (or languages) in which the participants have greater access is used to annotate the lessons', and yet, he continues that 'there is little exploratory use of "language" in the classroom' (89). Two exchanges in Martin (2005) between the teacher (T) in an English class in a primary classroom in a rural Malaysian community and the pupils (P) make this evident:

> T: *apa yang dia makan itu?* [what is he eating?]
> P: bread
> T: bread
> T: *apa itu?* [what's that?]
> P: *roti* [bread]
> T: *itu yang kita panggil* bread [that's what's called bread]
>
> (Martin, 2005: 80)

This teacher uses Malay to facilitate comprehension, and the students' responses are accepted in either English (as in the first exchange) or in Malay (as in the second). Teachers in post-colonial situations, teaching through the former colonial language and desperate because students are not learning, often use the students' home language practices to ensure the students' understandings of the content.

Bunyi (2005) has also documented how teachers in a Gĩkũyũ-speaking rural community in Nairobi failed to enforce the rule that no Gĩkũyũ be used. Bunyi describes the teachers' use of code-switching, not only to give meaning of lexical items or whole sentences, but also to carry out discipline, keep order and manage tasks. One teacher explains: '*Onaithuĩ arimũ nĩtũremagwo nĩgathĩkĩre watho ũcio. Onawe ũrĩ o mũndũ*' ['We teachers too are unable to obey the rule. Even you (the teacher) are human'] (133).

There is abundant empirical evidence that in all classrooms with bilingual learners, teachers and students move between 'languages' naturally to teach and learn (Creese and Martin, 2003; Gajo, 2007; Lin and Martin, 2005; Macaro, 2001; Martin-Jones, 1995). In fact, Arthur and Martin (2006) speak of the 'pedagogic validity of codeswitching' in these situations (197). Despite the evidence that moving between 'languages'

DOI: 10.1057/9781137385765

in education is an established practice of students and teachers and could be of pedagogical importance, these practices are considered non-legitimate.

Creese and Blackledge (2010) explain that code-switching 'becomes a pragmatic response to the local classroom context,' but is 'rarely institutionally endorsed or pedagogically underpinned' (105). Lemke (2002) raises an important question about the failure of schools in developing truly plurilingual students: 'Could it be that all our current pedagogical methods in fact make multilingual development more difficult than it need be, simply because we bow to dominant political and ideological pressures to keep "languages" pure and separate?' (85).

Many scholars are now answering the question posed by Lemke in the affirmative. For example, Gumperz and Cook-Gumperz (2005) have argued that schools need to purposefully create interactive spaces where it is safe to access all linguistic resources, rather than trying to keep the languages separate. Anton and DiCamilla (1998) have shown that using students' home languages in a foreign language classroom may facilitate the acquisition of a 'second' language. Speaking about 'dual language education' policies in the US, Fitts (2006) demonstrates how language separation is a mechanism that authorizes 'standard' English and Spanish, and 'illegitimizes the use of vernaculars' (339). In fact, the move in the US away from 'bilingual' programs to what are now called 'dual language' programs signals not only a political reaction against an increasingly bilingual reality, but also an attempt to only recognize bilingualism as additive, and to 'erase' the complex reality of US bilingual speakers (see García, 2009a, 2013, 2014a; García and Kleifgen, 2010). Lee et al. (2008) discuss how 'dual language education' classrooms in the US often dichotomize children as speakers of one or another language, thus thickening their language identities as speakers of an L1 and an L2, and limiting opportunities to be socialized to use both languages in one setting. They explain that 'the strict separation of the two languages for instructional purposes appears to be diminishing opportunities to use both codes as resources to problem-solve or as an indexical strategy' (90).

In 1990 Jacobson developed a bilingual education pedagogy in the United States that went against strict language separation, which he termed 'the concurrent approach.' Although the concurrent approach went against the separation of languages, it contained within it traditional conceptualizations of language and of language teaching. For example, teachers were taught to use code-switching strategically, but

DOI: 10.1057/9781137385765

only inter-sententially. Although the approach was never legitimized, it did raise questions of whether the separation of language approach was the only way to teach. In the section that follows we describe other alternative developments in education scholarship in which bilingualism in education is not simply seen as two parallel monolingualisms.

Promoting flexible languaging in teaching

The common assumption that only the 'target' language was to be used in language education programs, and of strict language separation, has become increasingly questioned as globalization has encouraged movement of people and information, shifting our conceptions of language use in ways described at the beginning of this book. Different scholars have referred to this more flexible languaging used to teach bilingual children by different terms.

Fu (2003) writes about the ways in which she uses a *bilingual process approach* to develop Chinese students' writing abilities in English:

> I believe thinking (reasoning and imagination) and the ability to organize ideas are equally, or even more, important than language skills in learning to write. If we let our students express themselves and present their ideas in their primary language, we give them opportunities to continue the development of their thinking. With this development uninterrupted, they are able to write well in a second language once they develop proficiency in it. (74)

Cummins (2007) supports *bilingual instructional strategies* as a way of promoting 'identities of competence among language learners from socially marginalized groups, thereby enabling them to engage more confidently with literacy and other academic work in both languages' (238). In his preface to Fu's *Writing Between Languages* (2009), Cummins discusses the recent shift in using bilingual instructional strategies in English-medium classes thereby 'opening up the pedagogical space in ways that legitimate the intelligence, imagination, and linguistic talents of ELL [English language learner] students' (xi). Although Cummins (2005) does not talk about translanguaging, he does name at least three 'bilingual pedagogical strategies' to fight against the 'two solitudes' of French and English in Canadian classrooms:

(a) systematic attention to cognate relationships across languages;
(b) creation of student-authored dual language books by means of translation from the initial language of writing to the L2; other multimedia

DOI: 10.1057/9781137385765

and multilingual projects can also be implemented (e.g., creation of IMovies, PowerPoint presentations, etc.);

(c) sister class projects where students from different language backgrounds collaborate using two or more languages (588).

Manyack (2004) shows the potential of *strategies of translation* in educating Latino students in an English immersion primary classroom. Translation is used in the first-grade classroom Manyack describes to include both students developing English, as well as those in the school who did not speak Spanish. In addition, strategies of translation enabled the writing of individual bilingual books.

Also supporting the teacher's ability to use students' language practices in language instruction, Macaro (2006) says: 'Taking away the bilingual teacher's right to codeswitch is like taking away the student's right to use a bilingual dictionary' (75). Macaro identifies five areas for which teachers report using the students' home languages in language instruction:

1   Building personal relationship with learners.
2   Giving complex procedural instructions for carrying out an activity.
3   Controlling pupils' behavior.
4   Translating and checking understanding in order to speed things up because of time pressures.
5   Teaching grammar explicitly. (69)

Transgressing dual language structures

Studies of student interaction in two-way dual language bilingual classrooms in the United States are increasingly showing the ways in which learners violate the strict language separation of the structure to appropriate knowledge. Angelova, Gunawardena and Volk (2006) show how first graders (6 years old) mediate their own and each other's language learning within and across languages. Despite the language separation policy of the two-way dual language bilingual classroom, peers repeat, paraphrase, translate, echo, clarify, scaffold, code-switch and communicate non-verbally among each other.

In a study of a fifth-grade dual language bilingual education classroom where 90 per cent of the students are Latinos (10 years old), Martín-Beltrán (2010) notes:

> Student interactions offer rich affordances for language learning when students are given the opportunity to draw on two or more languages simultaneously in dialogue with members of distinct linguistic communities as

DOI: 10.1057/9781137385765

they participate in joint activities ... The students' dual language use not only deepened metalinguistic analysis but also multiplied the language learning affordances within the interactions. (260)

Martín-Beltrán observes that 'languages can go back and forth symbiotically as meditational tools and objects of analysis within the same interaction' (256), as students work together to solve linguistic problems through what Swain and Lapkin (1998) call Language-Related-Episode (LRE). In these LREs, students talk about language, question the language or correct themselves or others. As the use of their home language practices mediate social interaction, distributed cognition and metalinguistic consciousness emerges, and thus there is more uptake from the learner, able to appropriate new language practices as their own. Martín-Beltrán describes:

> Their dialogue could be described as throwing a *metaphorical boomerang* across languages, when they began their metalinguistic analysis in language A, transferred this knowledge to analyze language B, then returned to language A with new insight and possibly a deeper level of analysis that had transformed their learning processes. (266, our emphasis)

In effect, this *metaphorical boomerang* of language use transforms the learners' thought processes, the artifact as assimilated and reconstructed by learners, as well as the sociocultural context or situation which brings about the change in social practice.

Transgressing the languages of literacy

Martínez (2010), Gort (2006) and Kibler (2010) examine the potential of using the students' home language practices specifically in teaching literacy. Martínez (2010) considers what he calls the use of 'Spanglish' as a literacy tool by sixth graders (approximately 11 years of age) in East Los Angeles. The use of the students' alternative language practices enabled their ability to shift voices for different audiences, as well as to communicate subtle shades of meaning in their writing. In a study of how writers who are at the beginning points of the bilingual continuum create texts, Gort (2006) shows how they use their full linguistic repertoire when creating texts. She says: 'These young writers drew on their dual language knowledge as they searched for ways to express themselves about things that mattered to them' (341). An important finding in this study is that these children developed 'spontaneous biliteracy' (Reyes, 2001); that is, they acquired literacy in Spanish and English without formal instruction

DOI: 10.1057/9781137385765

in Spanish. As in other studies, Gort shows that the children were apply-ing specific hypotheses and knowledge about language and literacy cross-linguistically to create texts in both languages (Edelsky, 1989; Escamilla et al., 2013; Manyak, 2000, 2004).

Kibler (2010) shows the potential of using students' home languages as affordances for each other. She describes how a bilingual secondary stu-dent's writing gets stronger and generates more details when a classmate utilizes his or her home language to discuss the ideas and the meaning. Kibler (2010) summarizes: 'It is clear that L1 use changes expectations for both the content and the "doing" of in-school writing, highlighting the fact that writing is shaped by classroom interaction' (132). In the case described by Kibler, students in secondary classrooms used their home language during writing activities to cognitively manage tasks (as cog-nitive affordance), as well as to position themselves in relation to their peers and teachers as experts or novices so as to affirm their multilingual identities as social affordance.

In their study of biliteracy development in English and Spanish from the start of schooling, Escamilla et al. (2013) argue that Latino children in the US are increasingly entering school as simultaneous bilinguals because they live in homes where varied language practices are used, and thus a sequential approach to biliteracy is not appropriate. The biliteracy approach they develop includes attention to cross-language connections for they acknowledge 'children's developing skills in Spanish and English as intertwined rather than belonging to separate linguistic systems' (10). Escamilla et al. add that children 'draw on all of their bilingual compe-tencies as they become biliterate ... ' (58).

All these scholars and studies show the dynamic language interactions of bilingual students in classrooms and the potential of this languaging dynamism for learning. And yet, these scholars still speak about L1, L2 and code-switching, signaling that there has not been a full shift in epistemologi-cal understandings about language, bilingualism and education in the ways in which translanguaging points. And yet, it has been precisely this new awareness of the power of this dynamic bilingualism (see Part I earlier) that has resulted in the uptake of the term *translanguaging* in language education scholarship and the new epistemologies about language and bilingualism that are reflected in the term. In Chapter 4 we explore the development of the use of the term translanguaging in education, in the face of new epistemolo-gies about language education, and discuss why a theory of translanguaging, rather than traditional ones of bilingualism, has the potential to transform educational practices, as well as the lives of bilingual children.

DOI: 10.1057/9781137385765

4
Translanguaging and Education

Abstract: *This chapter traces the development of a theory of translanguaging in education, from its Welsh beginnings, and its relationship to the important educational concepts of creativity and criticality. The chapter explicitly states why it is important to go from bilingualism in education to translanguaging in education, and the impact of this shift to transform monolingual, foreign/second language education and bilingual education structures.*

Keywords: bilingual education; creativity; criticality; Thirdspace; translanguaging

García, Ofelia, and Li Wei. *Translanguaging: Language, Bilingualism and Education.* Basingstoke: Palgrave Macmillan, 2014. DOI: 10.1057/9781137385765.

The development of translanguaging in education

As we said before, the term translanguaging was coined in Welsh by Cen Williams to refer to a teaching practice of deliberately changing the language of input and the language of output. Williams (2002) further clarifies that translanguaging in education refers to using one language to reinforce the other in order to increase understanding and in order to augment the *pupil's activity in both languages* (as cited in Lewis, Jones and Baker, 2012b: 40, our emphasis). Translanguaging, as used by Williams, refers to a pedagogic theory that involves students' learning of two languages through *a process* of deep cognitive bilingual engagement. Lewis, Jones and Baker (2012b) summarize Williams (1996) pedagogic theory saying:

> The process of translanguaging uses various cognitive processing skills in listening and reading, the assimilation and accommodation of information, choosing and selecting from the brain storage to communicate in speaking and writing. Thus, translanguaging requires a deeper understanding than just translating as it moves from finding parallel words to processing and relaying meaning and understanding. (644)

Colin Baker (2001) discusses four potential educational advantages to translanguaging:

1   It may promote a deeper and fuller understanding of the subject matter.
2   It may help the development of the weaker language.
3   It may facilitate home–school links and cooperation.
4   It may help the integration of fluent speakers with early learners.

Translanguaging thus goes beyond the simple use of a 'safe' practice just to understand the lesson, in the ways described by Martin (2005) or Hornberger and Chick (2001). Lewis, Jones and Baker (2012a,b), following Williams, point out that the cognitive processing involved in translanguaging is more relevant for *retaining and developing bilingualism*, rather than just for those at the initial stages of the bilingual continuum. As Colin Baker (2011) explains: 'To read and discuss a topic in one language, and then to write about it in another language, means that the subject matter has to be processed and "digested" ' (289). Translanguaging not only promotes a deeper understanding of content, but also develops the weaker language in relationship with the one that is more dominant. In addition, translanguaging facilitates the integration in classrooms of

DOI: 10.1057/9781137385765

students across the bilingual continuum (Lewis, Jones and Baker, 2012b). A five-year research project in Wales has determined that translanguaging was used as the only or dominant approach in approximately one-third of the 100 lessons observed (Lewis, Jones and Baker, 2013). In Wales, where bilingualism is mostly valued, translanguaging for the purposes of sustaining bilingual practices is moving to the educational mainstream.

Neurolinguists have begun to study translanguaging using event-related potentials (ERPs) that index semantic integration efforts in the brain. Recent research by Guillaume Thierry, as reported by Lewis, Jones and Baker (2012b), shows that semantic-relatedness is greater for objects learned in translanguaging sequences where the speaker encodes definitions in one language and retrieves related object names in the other language than for monolingual sequences. The suggestion is that because of cross-language semantic remapping translanguaging may be more effective for learning.

García's use of the Welsh-inspired term 'translanguaging' in *Bilingual Education in the 21st Century: A Global Perspective* (2009a) goes beyond the use of two separate autonomous languages in education, adopting the translanguaging lens that we have developed in Part I: 'translanguaging are *multiple discursive practices* in which bilingual engage in order to *make sense of their bilingual worlds*' (45, emphasis in original). Translanguaging, García says (2011a, 147), goes beyond code-switching and translation in education because it 'refers to the *process* by which bilingual students perform bilingually in the myriad multimodal ways of classrooms – reading, writing, taking notes, discussing, signing, etc.' (emphasis added). Translanguaging is not only a way to 'scaffold instruction, to make sense of learning and language; rather, translanguaging is part of the metadiscursive regime that students in the twenty-first century must perform' (García, 2011a: 147). Describing the work of the International Network of Public High Schools in the United States (public high schools for immigrant adolescents), García and Sylvan (2011) refer to the fact that students use 'diverse language practices for purposes of learning, and teachers use inclusive language practices for purposes of teaching' (397). In the context of US bilingual classrooms for immigrant students who are developing English, García and Kleifgen (2010) describe how educators often encourage those at the beginning points of the bilingual continuum to translanguage in order to think, reflect and extend their inner speech. García (2009b) describes the role of translanguaging in the process of developing students' bilingualism in the following way:

DOI: 10.1057/9781137385765

> Emergent bilinguals do not acquire a separate additional language, but develop and integrate new language practices into a complex dynamic bilingual repertoire in which translanguaging is both the supportive context and the communicative web itself. (n.p.)

In education, translanguaging is 'a process by which students and teachers engage in complex discursive practices that include ALL the language practices of ALL students in a class in order to develop new language practices and sustain old ones, communicate and appropriate knowledge, and give voice to new sociopolitical realities by interrogating linguistic inequality' (García and Kano, forthcoming).

Hornberger and Link (2012) explicitly connect translanguaging to Hornberger's *continua of biliteracy* (2003), enabling the potential 'to explicitly valorize all points along the continua of biliterate context, media, content, and development' (268). Hornberger's continua of biliteracy posits an L1–L2 continuum that addresses the complex relationship between the two languages. Hornberger (2005) adds:

> Bi/multilinguals' learning is maximized when they are allowed and enabled to draw from across all their existing language skills (in two+ languages), rather than being constrained and inhibited from doing so by monolingual instructional assumptions and practices. (607)

Translanguaging builds on Hornberger's important continua of biliteracy. By doing away with the distinctions between the 'languages' of bilinguals, translanguaging offers a way for students to draw on the diverse aspects of the Hornberger continua.

Drawing on ethnographic research in complementary schools in the United Kingdom, Creese and Blackledge (2010; also Blackledge and Creese, 2010) describe how the students' flexible bilingualism, their translanguaging, is used by teachers to convey ideas and to promote 'cross-linguistic transfer'. That is, as a *flexible bilingual pedagogy* (Blackledge and Creese, 2010), translanguaging offers learners the possibility of accessing academic content with the semiotic resources they bring, while acquiring new ones.

Translanguaging, creativity, criticality and transformations in education

The notion of translanguaging highlights two concepts that are fundamental to education, but that have hitherto been under-explored

DOI: 10.1057/9781137385765

dimensions of multilingualism, namely creativity and criticality (Li Wei, 2011a,b). As discussed in Chapter 2, *creativity* is the ability to choose between following and flouting the rules and norms of behavior, including the use of language. It is about pushing and breaking the boundaries between the old and the new, the conventional and the original and the acceptable and the challenging. *Criticality* refers to the ability to use available evidence appropriately, systematically and insightfully to inform considered views of cultural, social, political and linguistic phenomena, to question and problematize received wisdom, and to express views adequately through reasoned responses to situations. These two concepts are intrinsically linked: one cannot push or break boundaries without being critical; and the best expression of one's criticality is one's creativity. Translanguaging, as a socioeducational process, enables students to construct and constantly modify their sociocultural identities and values, as they respond to their historical and present conditions critically and creatively. It enables students to contest the 'one language only' or 'one language at a time' ideologies of monolingual and traditional bilingual classrooms.

Translanguaging in education also pays attention to the ways in which students combine different modes and media across social contexts and negotiate social identities. For example, Kenner (2004) reports on how bilingual/biliterate young children in the UK learn different writing systems (Chinese, Arabic and Spanish) at home, in complementary schools, and in the mainstream primary school. Her work illustrates how a focus on different modes, including the children's sets of linguistic resources, can foreground the different culture-specific ways multilingual children mesh the visual and actional modes (that is, make use of shape, size and location of symbols on the page, directionality, type of stroke) in the process of learning how to write in two languages. Moreover, such a focus shows the different ways multilingual children combine and juxtapose scripts as well as explore connections and differences between their available writing systems in their text making. By drawing on more than one set of linguistic and other modal resources to creatively construct bilingual texts in settings where multilingual communication was encouraged, Kenner argued that children could 'express their sense of living in multiple social and cultural worlds' (118).

Translanguaging in schools not only creates the possibility that bilingual students could use their full linguistic and semiotic repertoire to make meaning, but also that teachers would 'take it up' as a legitimate

DOI: 10.1057/9781137385765

pedagogical practice. Rather than just being a scaffolding practice to access content or language, translanguaging is *transformative* for the child, for the teacher and for education itself, and particularly for bilingual education. We start by considering why translanguaging as a theory of teaching and learning is different from traditional theories of bilingualism in education. Translanguaging offers an entry into systems of monolingual education that are in reality multilingual because of children's experiences with language practices other than those of schools. Translanguaging also has the potential to transform practices in bilingual education, as we discuss below.

Translanguaging, and not just bilingualism, in education

As the greater communication web enhanced by technology and globalization reveals the injustices suffered in schools by autochthonous, indigenous and immigrant language minorities, a way has to be found to pierce the monolingual bubble of schools for both non-dominant and dominant groups. Although bilingual education is spreading throughout the world, most language-minoritized children are still educated in monolingual programs where they remain silent and miseducated. And bilingual education programs, as we have seen, do not always offer ways of extending school-based practices with home-based ones. Translanguaging offers a way to do this by transgressing educational structures and practices, offering not just a navigational space that crosses discursive boundaries, but a space in which competing language practices, as well as knowledge and doing, emerging from both home and school are *brought together*. It is precisely the bringing together of all students' languaging and doing that generates new knowledge and learning, as well as new languaging and texts. That is, translanguaging *transgresses and destabilizes* language hierarchies, and at the same time *expands and extends* practices that are typically valued in school and in the everyday world of communities and homes. As we said in Chapter 2 of this book, translanguaging relates to Borges' Aleph – the sum total of language practices that transform a present space with historicity, creativity, criticality and power.

Figure 4.1 depicts translanguaging as expanding, leveraging and transcending home and school practices, in a Borgean Aleph. That is,

DOI: 10.1057/9781137385765

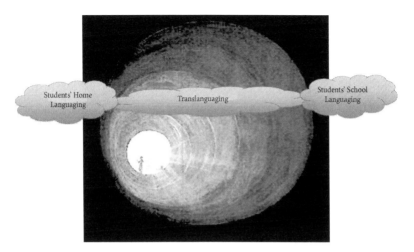

FIGURE 4.1   *Translanguaging in education*

translanguaging requires an epistemological change in which students' everyday languaging and school languaging is expanded and integrated, and in so doing blends ways of knowing which are traditionally found in different spaces.

Translanguaging, then, goes beyond just tapping linguistic 'funds of knowledge' (Moll, Díaz, Estrada and Lopes, 1992), traditionally understood as the student 'L1' when speaking an 'L2.' Instead, translanguaging validates the fact that bilingual students' language practices are not separated into an L1 and an L2, or into home language and school language, instead transcending both (Moje, Díaz, Estrada and Lopes, 2004). Beyond the idea of *transfer* (Cummins, 1979), which points to the effortless transmission of skills from one language to another, translanguaging refers to bilingual speakers *leveraging* (Michaels, 2005) their entire linguistic semiotic repertoire in meaning-making, and in the process transforming it as well. Beyond bilingualism in education, which sees the two languages as separately performed, translanguaging in education encourages bilingual performances that in so doing enable students to move simultaneously along the continuum of two socially constructed languages according to standards of the community and the home, as well as those of school. This leveraging of linguistic semiotic resources in meaning-making is important for all bilingual students, whether they're situated at the beginning points of the bilingual continuum or whether they're further along the continuum. And it is a way of developing their

DOI: 10.1057/9781137385765

critical consciousness, the conscientization that involves a continual reading of the word and the world (Freire, 1974).

As we will show, the *process* of translanguaging in schools many times results in a *product* that is cast as being in one language or another. The question then is whether there is a difference between the traditional understanding of valuing students' home language as a resource in learning and the position for which we're arguing here. Translanguaging is viewed here as the process of tapping a single expanded linguistic repertoire that students and teachers use to make meaning and to learn. The difference between taking a bilingual approach to education or a translanguaging approach to education, although subtle, is transformational.

As we have said in Part I, translanguaging transforms traditional notions of language, bilingualism and education. In the next section we consider how translanguaging transforms educational structures and practices beyond those in traditional monolingual, bilingual and second/foreign language programs.

Transgressing monolingual and bilingual education through translanguaging

As national education systems have taken on more responsibility for educating all children, and not just those of dominant majorities, translanguaging is beginning to be used, at times, to transgress monolingual education structures. And as bilingual education has increasingly incorporated children with different languaging practices, translanguaging has disrupted traditional bilingual education structures. That is why today description of traditional models of bilingual education are giving way to more complex descriptions of factors and variables, such as the one given by Baetens Beardsmore (2009) or the model proposed as the Continua of Multilingual Education by Cenoz (2009) discussed in Chapter 3. Translanguaging in classrooms is precisely a way of working in the gap between, on the one hand, the global designs of nation-states and their monoglossic education systems, and on the other, the local histories of peoples who language differently. So why translanguaging and not simply bilingualism in education? The answers to this question considered below all amount to saying that translanguaging is a more encompassing and transformative concept than bilingualism because it transforms monolingual education, bilingual education and foreign/second language education programs.

DOI: 10.1057/9781137385765

Translanguaging and monolingual education

On the one hand, adopting translanguaging would mean that monolingual education would cease to exist. Even if the lessons were carried out 'officially' in one language, adopting translanguaging would mean that the language practices of ALL students would be used as a resource for learning. All teachers in all classrooms would understand that their students' linguistic repertoires never completely match their own or each others', and that having students use all their language practices would be beneficial for learning, for deep cognitive engagement and for development and expansion of new language practices, including standard ones used for academic purposes. As Gutiérrez, Baquedano-López and Alvarez (2001) have demonstrated, students in all classrooms today demonstrate diversity and interplay between linguistic features and literacy practices. Translanguaging transgresses monolingual education and monolingual teaching.

Translanguaging and bilingual education

On the other hand, translanguaging for bilingual education would mean that the students' entire linguistic repertoire, and not just one or another language as defined by nation-states, would be recognized and accepted. Beyond the languages used in bilingual and multilingual education, other language practices inscribed in the students' bodies would be leveraged. In this way students engage cognitively and expand not only their language practices to encompass differences, but also take up socially relevant practices, including standard language practices for academic purposes. That is, bilingual students across the continuum of bilingualism would be able to slide along the range of language practices that make up their lives.

In addition, for bilingual education, adopting a translanguaging lens means that we would build flexibility within strict language education policies to enable children to make meaning by engaging their entire linguistic repertoire and expanding it. As we said before, many bilingual education types, and especially immersion and two-way dual language programs, pride themselves in controlling carefully the language use within the different spaces they construct. The argument is made that children should only practice languages as if they belonged to different nation-states or different speech communities. But today language has been deterritorialized, as diasporic communities interact with other communities of practice in what, as we said before, Mary Louise Pratt (1991) has called contact zones. In this more dynamic world of interaction, real and virtual, students need practice and engagement in translanguaging,

DOI: 10.1057/9781137385765

as much as they need practice of standard features used for academic purposes.

Another argument made in many bilingual education programs that insist on separating languages strictly is that the minoritized language needs to be protected from the dominant one. In some ways, this follows Joshua A. Fishman's concept of *diglossia* which claims that, 'socially patterned bilingualism can exist as a stabilized phenomenon only if there is functional differentiation between two languages' (Fishman, Cooper and Ma, 1971: 560). But a translanguaging theory, as we've been arguing throughout this book, goes beyond the static definition of language as autonomous and pure, and as used 'originally' by a specific group of people whose identity depends on this.

Translanguaging adopts a *transglossic* position (García, 2013, 2014a) that goes beyond the concept of *language maintenance* and poses that language practices need to be sustained (not simply maintained), and always in interaction with the social context in which they operate. García (2011b: 7) explains the difference between the concept of *language sustainability* in contrast to language maintenance and says:

> The concept of sustainability contains in its core the grappling with social, economic and environmental conditions by which systems remain diverse and productive over time. That is, the concept of sustainability is dynamic and future-oriented, rather than static and past-oriented. Language sustainability refers to renewing past language practices to meet the needs of the present while not compromising those of future generations. Thus, the sustainability of languaging is a *new* copy of the past, a dynamic relocalization in space and time, a fertile performative mimesis that brings us to a creative emergence, a new and generative becoming. (for more on this idea, see Pennycook (2010))

Bilingual education programs must aim to both sustain the language practices of minoritized communities and redress the language inequalities that have been created through the invention of separate and autonomous languages – one dominant and spoken by insiders, the other minoritized, heritage and always the language of outsiders. To separate languages and identities is indeed to segregate and maintain bilingual language minorities as the Other. Instead, we must aim for sustainability of the complex language practices of bilinguals in functional interrelationship with the social and academic context in which they are performed.

The exigencies of learning and of using language have become more complex today. Both bilingual education and 'foreign' and 'second'

DOI: 10.1057/9781137385765

language education programs in the 20th century emphasized communicative skills. Today, however, the emphasis is on the development of critical thinking skills and deep comprehension. For example, in the United States, 46 states (as of this writing) have for the first time adopted Common Core State Standards that focus on complex use of language and literacy (see García and Flores, 2014). Schools cannot afford to focus on just developing linguistic communicative skills to later teach students how to use these skills to learn and think. And a just education cannot solely use languaging associated with a constructed autonomous language, before introducing other language practices, as was often done in the bilingual education programs of the past (for example, immersion bilingual education or transitional bilingual education programs where only one language was used for a period of time before the other language was introduced). If languaging and knowing are constitutive, as we said before, then schools must pay attention from the beginning to getting students to use all their language practices to think critically and act on the world. But this, of course, cannot happen without translanguaging, for students cannot engage in meaningful discussion, comprehension or designing and redesigning of texts with only a set of emergent language practices. Instead, all the child's language and semiotic practices must be put in the service of making meaning. Even if schools only value certain 'standard academic' language practices, those cannot emerge except in interrelationship with others with which children have practice making meaning at home, in the community and within themselves. Translanguaging brings us closer to the Aleph of language practices. Translanguaging thus also transgresses traditional bilingual education structures and practices.

A theory of translanguaging offers educators a non-competitive perspective between 'languages' of instruction. Despite the early efforts of Cummins (1979) in challenging that there is a separate proficiency in L1 and in L2, teachers have not been convinced that as Cummins (1981) argues, 'one can better inflate the L2 balloon by blowing into the L1 balloon' (23). Many educators continue to believe that instruction through the home language does not contribute much to development of a new language. But by doing away with the distinction between an L1 and an L2, a translanguaging theory offers educators the possibility of understanding that bilingual language practices do not compete with each other because there is but one system from which students select appropriate features. Reviewing Figure 1.1 would help readers understand this

DOI: 10.1057/9781137385765

perspective. A translanguaging theory in education views the incorporation of the students' full linguistic repertoire as simply the only way to go about developing language practices valued in school, as well as to educate.

Despite our valuing of the translanguaging of bilinguals as one linguistic repertoire, we agree that bilingual education programs must also build spaces where certain language practices or others are sometimes expected. This is what dominant society and government schools and their assessment mechanisms continue to require, and thus, it is important to give students an opportunity to engage in these practices. In this regard, we agree with the position of Janks (2000) when speaking about critical literacy:

> Critical literacy has to take seriously the ways in which meaning systems are implicated in reproducing domination and it has to provide access to dominant languages, literacies and genres while simultaneously using diversity as a productive resource for redesigning social futures and for changing the horizon of possibility. (178)

Bilingual education programs must help students become critically conscious in a Freirean sense and develop the tools to engage with the relationship between language and power so as to transform their future possibilities. But at the same time, as Freire (1973) has pointed out, it is important to teach students to command the language practices of dominant societies in order to engage with transforming society. Thus García (2009a) argues:

> While it is important to put the minority language alongside the majority language, thus ensuring for it a place in powerful domains, it is important to preserve a space, although not a rigid or static place, in which the minority language does not compete with the majority language. (301)

But within those separate spaces, schools must also construct *translanguaging spaces*, spaces where, as Li Wei (2011b) has proposed, children are given agency to act linguistically by being both *creative* and *critical*, and where teachers encourage those actions. In this translanguaging space, children's language practices are brought together in ways that not only develop an extended bilingual repertoire capable of deeply involving them cognitively, but also a more sophisticated metalinguistic awareness that would enable them to negotiate these extended linguistic repertoires. That is, in these translanguaging spaces linguistically diverse students

DOI: 10.1057/9781137385765

are able to co-construct their language expertise, recognize each other as resources, and act on their knowing and doing. This builds, as we will see in the next section, on Bhabha's notion of Third space (1994) and of the Thirdspace of Soja (1996) described in Chapter 2.

Building thirdspaces: beyond foreign/second language and bilingual education

Whereas, as we saw above, bilingual education program types respond to strict language policies that control how language is used, there are new types of educational programs emerging that structure themselves within this translanguaging space. We discuss here two such programs. One example is the secondary programs for immigrant newcomers to the United States that García and Sylvan (2011) have described. In these programs students are given the agency to negotiate their linguistic and meaning-making repertoires. That is, the locus of control of the language rests with the students, as they move to expand their home language practices to include those in English for academic use. In so doing, they rely especially on peers and resources such as iPads and Google Translate, and certainly not solely on the teacher who rarely shares all the language practices of the students. The teacher then becomes the facilitator, generating opportunities for language use, and seeing herself not as the linguistic authority, but as another language learner. García and Sylvan (2011: 393–394) describe these classrooms:

> Students are...talking, arguing, trying to make their points and collaborating on a project together. In so doing, they're using different language practices, including those they bring from home. ... You find students using bilingual dictionaries (both electronic and paper)...Multiple conversations are happening at multiple times in many languages with occasional breaks in the 'chaos' for the teacher to explain a concept or practice a skill collectively that students immediately apply in the work they are doing. Students have considerable choice in how they arrive at the final project, including the language they use to negotiate, and the eventual form that the project takes, but activity guides and rubrics (often collectively designed between teachers and students) establish parameters in which students operate. ... Students depend on one another to share their experiences, knowledge, perspectives, and understandings of the text, so they teach each other. The teacher is not the only 'expert' in the room and considerable control is handed over to the students. Content is made accessible because students work on figuring out the content, language and implications together. Students are constantly

DOI: 10.1057/9781137385765

asked to 're-present' the information they are reading and studying, and to discuss it collectively.

García and Kleifgen (2010) have called these programs *dynamic bi/ plurilingual education*. These educational spaces of negotiation and contact rarely exist in established school systems, and we have found them only at the secondary level, and only for language-minoritized students whose bilingualism is emerging. Because of the nature of schooling, translanguaging is used in these classrooms mostly to scaffold instruction so that students develop features associated with standard English for academic purposes. Translanguaging is valued then because of its potential to educate the children in English, more than for its capacity to sustain the students' own languaging.

The exigencies of global communication, the failures associated with foreign/second language education, the neglect of autochthonous regional minorities, and the absence of provisions for bilingualism in education for immigrants have led many European countries to develop what are called CLIL (Content and Language Integrated Learning) programs. These programs are in effect bilingual programs in which an additional language, whether a foreign language or a community language, is used to learn and teach both content and language. Despite the fact that many CLIL programs teaching foreign languages or community languages do so following traditional understandings and structures, Coyle, Hood and Marsh (2010) make clear that there is space within CLIL for 'bilingual blended instruction involving code-switching between languages' (15). They describe:

> For example, sometimes one language might be used for outlining and summarizing the main points, and the other for the remaining lesson functions. Alternatively, the two different languages may be used for specific types of activity. … Some learners may use a textbook in the first language when doing homework in order to build confidence and check comprehension; other learners may ask for explanations from the teacher in a particular language; beginner CLIL learners may use their L1 to speak to the teacher when problem solving, but the CLIL teachers will answer questions and support learners in the vehicular language. (16)

Although these practices are described as code-switching, Coyle, Hood and Marsh (2010) place these practices within a translanguaging framework, defining translanguaging as 'a systematic shift from one language to another for specific reasons' (16). This definition of translanguaging

DOI: 10.1057/9781137385765

is closer to the Welsh original definition described at the beginning of this chapter rather than the one we're proposing here. However, this new acceptance of translanguaging in CLIL programs signals another promising space.

Translanguaging has the potential to change the nature of learning, as well as of teaching. In Chapter 5 we consider how students use translanguaging to learn, even when a translanguaging space is not officially available. That is, we look at how learners open up their own translanguaging spaces and find their Aleph in the Borgean sense of a place that encompasses, without confusion, their entire selves as learners, and their language and cultural practices. But again, we caution the reader that these translanguaging educational spaces are found today mostly in the education of students at the beginning points of the bilingual continuum. We then turn, in Chapter 6, to translanguaging to teach; that is, translanguaging as a pedagogy, a less-understood and less-developed area.

DOI: 10.1057/9781137385765

5
Translanguaging to Learn

Abstract: *Chapter 5 turns to how translanguaging is used by students to learn. We develop here the concept of pupil-directed translanguaging. After a discussion of its meaning, the chapter presents cases of how translanguaging is used by kindergarteners who are at the beginning stages of the bilingual continuum, and by bilingual students in order to write.*

Keywords: bilingual education; kindergarten; learning and bilingualism; translanguaging; writing and bilingualism

García, Ofelia, and Li Wei. *Translanguaging: Language, Bilingualism and Education*. Basingstoke: Palgrave Macmillan, 2014. DOI: 10.1057/9781137385765.

Students' use of translanguaging

Developing new language practices, especially academic ones, is not easy for learners. Learning new ways of languaging is more difficult than just learning new subject content in school because as A. L. Becker (1995) has said, it also involves learning 'a new way of being in the world' (227). If language constitutes us, then adding to a linguistic and semiotic repertoire means that we acquire not only new ways of speaking and acting, of languaging, but also of being, of knowing and of doing. For new languaging to be learned, much more is needed than just picking it up as in the 'acquisition' promoted by communicative language teaching, or learned as a system of structures as in grammar-translation methods. New language practices can only emerge in interrelationship with old ones, without competing or threatening an already established sense of being that languaging constitutes. Norton (2000) has called this desire to participate in learning, *investment.* Learners have complex social histories and multiple desires. To invest in learning new language practices some things are needed. On the one hand, learners need a secure sense of self that allows them to appropriate new language practices as they engage in a continuous becoming. On the other, learners must be able to cognitively engage with learning and to act on learning. That is, it is not enough simply to listen and take in forms or to output new forms. It is important to engage and interact socially and cognitively in the learning process in ways that produce and extend the students' languaging and meaning-making. Translanguaging is, as we have said, important to mediate students' identities, but also complex cognitive activities.

Translanguaging is also important for students to embrace *positioning,* which according to Davies and Harré (1990) is 'the discursive process whereby selves are located in conversations as observably and subjectively coherent participants in jointly produced story lines' (48). Language and literacy production cannot be reduced to simple techniques that are cognitively taken in by individuals. Instead, they are the product of positioning of students within social/political economies. Students are constantly experiencing successes and failures as *habitus* (Bourdieu, 1991); that is, school success and failure is created through a social process that guides behavior and thinking. It is through meaningful participation in the act of learning enabled by translanguaging that bilingual students can create for themselves identities that are also

DOI: 10.1057/9781137385765

academic (Palmer, 2008), and thus invest in learning. Translanguaging enables even emergent bilinguals to model forms of knowing and talking for others (Fitts, 2009) and to serve as 'language brokers' to other learners (Lee, Hill-Bonnet and Raley, 2011; Orellana, 2009; Orellana and Reynolds, 2008).

Translanguaging not only allows for shuttling between acts of language that are socially and educationally constructed as being separate, but integrates bilingual acts in ways that reflect the unified constitution of the learner. That is, translanguaging allows us to shed the concept of *transfer* that Cummins so long ago introduced to the field of bilingual education and to adopt a conceptualization of *integration* of language practices in *the person of the learner* (as we saw in Figure 1.1). Translanguaging goes beyond having to acquire and learn new language structures, rather it develops the integration of new language practices into one linguistic repertoire that is available for the speaker to be, know and do, and that is in turn produced in the complex interactions of bilingual speakers. Rather than learning a new separate 'second language', learners are engaged in appropriating new languaging that makes up their own unique repertoire of meaning-making resources. The language practices then don't belong to the school or to the home; the languaging is that of the learner, his or her own being, knowing and doing, as it emerges through social interaction.

If languaging is being, doing and knowing, then it stands to reason that learners cannot appropriate language practices without simultaneously also knowing. The development of new language practices are acts of knowing and doing. For those who are still developing new language practices; that is, for emergent bilingual students, knowledge cannot be accessed except through language practices with which they're already familiar. In turn, language practices cannot be developed except through the students' existing knowledge. Thus, translanguaging enables emergent bilinguals to enter into a text that is encoded through language practices with which they're not quite familiar. At the same time, translanguaging enables students to truly show what they know. Furthermore, the more students know about a text, the more they can 'language' and make meaning.

Translanguaging refers to the flexibility of bilingual learners to take control of their own learning, to self-regulate when and how to language, depending on the context in which they're being asked to perform.

DOI: 10.1057/9781137385765

Williams (2012) refers to this in the classroom as 'natural translanguaging', and gives examples of its use by students in writing or in oral work carried out in pairs or small groups to make sense of content. Lewis, Jones and Baker (2012a) call it *pupil-directed translanguaging*. This means, for example, that when bilinguals have to find new information by reading or speaking to others, they can language and use meaning-making resources that are not found in the classroom or lesson and with which teachers may not be familiar. Self-regulated learning emphasizes independence by students who monitor and regulate their knowledge and actions to acquire information, expand expertise and self-improve (Paris and Paris, 2001). Translanguaging strategies promote a high sense of self-efficacy, as students self-regulate their learning (Velasco and García, 2013). Embedded in this practice is the belief that learning is not a product, but *a process*.

According to sociocultural theory (Vygotsky, 1978), knowledge is acquired interpersonally, that is, in relationships with others and the world, before it becomes internalized. And thus, translanguaging is also important for metatalk (talk about talk), metacognition (talk about the task), and whispered private speech (Kibler, 2010), all essential for learning. By using translanguaging learners can extend their zone of proximal development (Lantolf, 2000).

Swain and Lapkin (2000) found that the use of the students' home language served three main functions. On the one hand, it moved the task along because it established a joint understanding by the students. It also allowed the learners to focus attention on vocabulary and grammatical items. Finally, it enhanced interpersonal interaction.

When university students who are developing English were asked to complete a text reconstruction task and a short joint composition task and were allowed to use their home languages, Storch and Wigglesworth (2003) found that students translanguaged mainly for task management and task clarification. Students reported that the use of their home language was useful to argue a point, and to provide each other with definitions of difficult vocabulary and explanations of grammar. The following three sections describe the translanguaging of students as they make meaning of their learning. The first case is that of kindergarteners in the US as they make sense of a new language; the second case is that of a student who translanguages in writing; and the third case is an analysis of how students use translanguaging to develop writing.

DOI: 10.1057/9781137385765

Kindergarteners using translanguaging[1]

Many scholars have convincingly shown how students themselves use translanguaging in order to learn and make sense of their world, even when teachers do not set up instructional situations to do so. In a study of a two-way dual language bilingual kindergarten, García (2011c) describes how translanguaging is used by children (5–6 years old) who enter school speaking what the school considers to be only English or only Spanish. Although there is a Spanish language teacher and an English language teacher who teach children in separate rooms where only one language is supposed to be used, these young kindergarteners use translanguaging for six metafunctions, as they develop their bilingualism:

1   To mediate understandings among each other;
2   To co-construct meaning of what the other is saying;
3   To construct meaning within themselves;
4   To include others;
5   To exclude others; and
6   To demonstrate knowledge.

The most prevalent use of translanguaging by these children was to co-construct meaning, both with others and within themselves. One day, for example, a young emergent bilingual boy is having his snack next to a more experienced bilingual girl. The Spanish-speaking boy looks out of the window and sees that it is raining, so he says to himself: '*Está lloviendo mucho*'. [It is raining a lot.] But as he looks around the table where he is snacking, he realizes that his classmates speak English, so he says: 'Look it's washing. There's washing *afuera*' [outside]. The bilingual girl kindly asks him, '*¿Está lloviendo?*' [Is it raining?] And then, she says to him, so that the other monolingual English-speaking children understand him: 'Raining'. At which point, the boy repeats, 'Raining' (10/19/2007, García, 2011c: 47). The boy had no word for 'raining', and used 'washing'. Translanguaging enabled the boy to communicate with others, as well as acquire the lexical item that he needed without any intervention from the teacher. Translanguaging in this interaction enabled the learning to take place.

Another time, the English teacher has taken the emergent bilingual children outside for an English as a Second Language lesson. The teacher is showing them the trees and comparing them, and says, as she points to different trees: 'This tree is bigger. That tree is smaller.' A young girl who is sitting on the ground next to García, tries it out under her breath: 'This tree is *grander*' (9/23/2007, García, 2011c: 50). Her use of '*grander*' is an example of translanguaging, a way of articulating and transforming thinking into artifactual form and thus of making it available as a source of further reflection (Swain, 2006). Inner or private speech has been shown to mediate thinking in progress and is key to learners' understandings of complex concepts (DiCamilla and Antón, 2004). *Grander* is also an example of how emergent bilinguals use their existing features to construct new ones, in this case the lexical item from Spanish, *grande*, with the morphological item for the comparative in English that she's learning, *-er*. The girl is activating her entire linguistic repertoire to learn, as well as creating new meanings.

At another time, a bilingual Latino boy translanguages to include the researcher who is sitting by his side (García), the English-speaking Teacher Assistant and the child's inner speech. This occurs in the English classroom. The bilingual boy is playing with an 'Etch-A-Sketch' Board – a drawing toy that creates lineographic images by displacing aluminium powder on the back of the screen – as he waits for a worksheet. We divide this monologue into four fragments (A–D) in order to do the analysis that follows.

A. *First interaction with the Etch-A-Sketch and García*

{Pablo speaks to García, as she sits quietly next to him}

Esto es magic. Yo puedo hacer magic. *Mira, se borró todo, y aquí está.*

[This is magic. I can do magic. Look, it was all erased, and here it is.]

Es magic...... *Mira que es* magic. *Y aquí está.*

[It's magic..... Look, it's magic. And here it is!]

Mira, son papeles. Y los encerraron aquí, pa' que los hagamos.

[Look, they're papers. And they put them in here, so that we can do them.]

I just erased it with my hand.

B. *Interaction with worksheet and Assistant Teacher*

{Pablo turns to the English-speaking Assistant Teacher who is distributing worksheets}

Can I do this with pencil? {meaning the worksheets}

I need some. I need this one. I could write......

C. *Interaction with worksheet and García*

{He then turns to García}

Mira, ¿quieres ver?

[Look, do you want to see?]

DOI: 10.1057/9781137385765

Éste no se borra con la mano.
> [You don't erase this with your hand.]

Y esto lo vamos a llevar a mi casa.
> [And this we're going to take home.]

D. Interaction with worksheet and himself
> {Speaks to himself, as he writes his name on the worksheet}

¡Ay, qué mal! Es que siempre lo hago mal.
> [Oh, so bad! It's that I always do it wrong.]
> {Speaking to himself again because he didn't put his name on the paper.}

I forgot my name.

Se me olvidó mi nombre.
> [I forgot my name.] (10/09/2007, García, 2011c: 51–2)

In this exchange, where the child is not being evaluated by the teacher for speaking one or the other language, the boy strategically uses his entire language repertoire. To interact with García (A and C) he selects features associated with Spanish, except for the important lexical item, 'magic'. With the Assistant Teacher (B), he selects features of English. With himself (D), he selects both, showing his comfort with all the features in his repertoire, as well as his competence in both languages, as socially constructed. But besides the interlocutor, also important are the tools or affordances that students use. With the Etch-A-Sketch, everything is 'magic' because he can erase it with his hand. Although his explanation about how the Etch-A-Sketch works is simplistic – pieces of paper that were put inside the board – the magic is that he can manipulate them because they were put there *'pa' que los hagamos'*. The fact that he can manipulate the papers and draw different realities means he is in charge because the papers are inside the board so that the child could 'do them'. The worksheet, however, is totally the opposite. You have to do it in pencil, only one way. You can't erase it and it will be surveilled by teachers. You also have to take it home where it will be further surveilled by parents. All of a sudden, the magic is gone, and all the child can say is that he always does it wrong, and that he forgot his name. Like the papers in the Etch-A-Sketch, his language practices come in and out, as he erases and weaves different language practices and linguistic subjectivities. But when the practices are controlled, as when he has to write in English only on the worksheet, he can't even write his name because 'siempre lo hago mal'. The boy's monologue serves as a metaphor of how school often constrains the languaging,

DOI: 10.1057/9781137385765

knowing and doing possibilities of learners, limiting their capacities to remain flexible, creative, critical, able to erase and bring back, able to experiment and take risks. You can't erase schoolwork that is always being evaluated.

What is interesting about the translanguaging of these very young learners is that whether they were emergent bilinguals or experienced bilinguals, they were not shy about using their entire language repertoire to make meaning, successfully communicating across 'languages' and 'modes' by combining all the multimodal semiotic signs at their disposal. Translanguaging always included linguistic signs from their growing repertoire, accompanied by gestures, pointing, physical imitations, noises, drawings and onomatopoeic words. Although in this class of five-year-olds, kindergarteners translanguage orally, the next two cases consider how writers translanguage, as well as the potential of translanguaging in developing writing.

Using translanguaging in writing

One of the most influential aspects of schooling is the development of literacy. Written-linguistic modes of meaning are intricately bound up not only with other visual, audio and spatial semiotic systems (Kress, 2003), but also with languaging practices that vary depending on situations, sociocultural contexts and complex social interactions (Street, 1993). Martin-Jones and Jones (2001) proposed the term *multilingual literacies* to refer to the multiplicity of individual and group repertoires and the varied communicative purposes for which groups draw on and combine language practices. García, Bartlett and Kleifgen (2007) speak about *pluriliteracy practices* to emphasize that literacy practices are inter-related and flexible, and have equal value, that is, translanguaging is important for literacy development because students develop the agency to use their entire semiotic system.

In examining the narrative writing of a bilingual graduate student by the name of Buthainah, Canagarajah (2011a) describes how in English writing she uses Arabic words and script, emoticons, elongations of words for auditory effects, italics, Islamic art and creative turns of phrase like 'storms of thoughts stampede'. Canagarajah (2011a) identifies four strategies that Buthainah uses in what he calls 'codemeshing':

1   Recontextualization strategies, as she gauges the context to figure out whether she could use codemeshing.

DOI: 10.1057/9781137385765

2   Voice strategies, by which she makes textual space for her linguistic resources.

3   Interactional strategies, which give her the confidence in her identity and background to draw from them as resources, as she negotiates meaning on an equal footing with readers.

4   Textualization strategies, as she focuses on the rhetorical effect on her readers and the persuasive appeal of her writing.

Translanguaging enables Buthainah to mediate the cognitively complex activity of writing, while she positions herself in relation to her audience and teacher as the expert, able to negotiate her multilingual identity. Canagarajah (2011a: 410) concludes: 'Multilinguals align words with other features of the ecology to produce meaning'. Translanguaging is the web that supports the students' literacy development. At the same time, Buthainah's actions are transformed and undergo resemiotization (Scollon and Scollon, 2004), as her creativity and criticality are unleashed through the process of translanguaging. In the next section we describe how bilingual students at different points of the continuum use translanguaging to reflect on their writing, using the case of Japanese American students.

Using translanguaging to write and read[2]

Students at different points of the bilingual continuum seem to have different tendencies in their use of translanguaging to learn. In a study by García and Kano (forthcoming) that used translanguaging as pedagogy (more on this below), the emergent bilinguals who were at the beginning points of the continuum tended to use translanguaging as *support*, and sometimes to *expand* their understandings, whereas those at the more advanced points of the continuum, the experienced bilinguals, used translanguaging more for their own *enhancement*. That is, for those at the beginning points of the bilingual continuum translanguaging *creates* the voice and knowledge through *support and expansion* of what they already know how to say and do. But more experienced bilinguals *enhance* their existing practices through translanguaging, accommodating them and sharpening what they know how to say and do. We do not want to imply here that one type of translanguaging or translanguager is better than the other, for all bilingual students use translanguaging for purposes of enhancement, support and expansion. But we want to distinguish between those students who are still in the beginning

DOI: 10.1057/9781137385765

process of acquiring the additional language and those who have had more experience or time with this process, and the *tendencies* that they have, as learners, in the use of translanguaging. García and Kano have referred to these different leanings by saying that emergent bilinguals usually display a *dependent translanguaging* pattern, whereas experienced bilinguals tend to use a more *independent translanguaging* pattern. We warn, however, that the reality is much more complex and that bilingual students at all points of the continuum use translanguaging at times for support, expansion and enhancement.

When Kano asked Satomi, a girl whose English was developing, about her strategies for reading in English, she said:

> 英語で、わかんないところだけ、日本語を見てました。
>
> *[In English, I was reading corresponding passages in the Japanese language whenever I didn't understand it in English.]*

In other words, Satomi, who came to the US from Japan at the age of 12, was using the Japanese text as a *scaffold* to understand the English text.

Haruka, also an emergent bilingual who lived in Singapore, Hong Kong and Japan, before arriving in the US, is shown a video clip of herself working on an English vocabulary exercise in which she has to come up with synonyms. She's asked what language process she used to accomplish the task. Her answer reveals her use of translanguaging not simply as support, but as *expander*. She says:

> そのときは日本語で考えてました...あの、思いつかなくて、やっぱり日本語でどんどんことばが出てきちゃったので。それに関しては日本語でした。[同義語練習問題の例] 'use up'っていうことばがあって、それ、'消費'って　思い出したら、'consume'が出て来たんで。そういうふうに日本語を使ってました。
>
> *[I was thinking in Japanese at the time.... I couldn't think of synonyms in English because Japanese words kept shooting through my mind one after another. So, I depended on my Japanese. [For example], we had 'use up' among the list. When I understood the word in Japanese ('消費'), an English word 'consume' came through my mind. This way, I used the Japanese language for the task.]*

Although Haruka was also an emergent bilingual, her contact with many cultures in Singapore and Hong Kong has given her more experience with translanguaging. She understands how she has one linguistic repertoire in which words keep 'shooting through her mind'. She's unable to 'turn off' features from the other language as she performs the language that is being required, but she understands that this is precisely her resource. She doesn't suppress it, but instead leverages it to perform the English

DOI: 10.1057/9781137385765

language task that is required at that moment. Both Satomi and Haruka tend to show a *dependent translanguaging pattern* as learners.

In contrast, Yuji, a more experienced bilingual, recounts how he made the best use of his bilingual abilities, using both languages to research because he wanted to get the best information. He recalls how he used both languages to prepare an essay:

今年の作文なんですけど、携帯電話が良いか悪いか、でリサーチをしたとき、日本語のものも英語のものも両方使いました...携帯電話が有益かどうか、日本語でやってみて、で日本語のリサーチを取って、英語でも、って英語のやつも取って、でそれを二つ使いました...両方のことばで調べてみて、一番良いのを使おうと思って。

[*This year, when I was doing research on the pros and cons about cell phones, I used materials both in Japanese and English..... I searched for the articles in Japanese on whether cell phones were beneficial, and I took some of them. Then I did the same thing in English. I ended up using the materials in both languages..... I searched in both languages in order to get the best ones available.*]

Yuji is an active translanguager, using every opportunity he has to develop his bilingual abilities. Yuji was born in Canada, moved to the US at the age of 4 and has never lived in Japan, and yet he speaks Japanese confidently. Yuji reveals his strategy to develop his Japanese:

英語ではこう言う、で、日本語ではこう言う、っていうのは時々考えてます..授業中とか、たまに先生のいうことばを日本語に変えてみたりすることはあります。

[*Sometimes, I think of a word in English and another word in Japanese that has the same meaning.... I sometimes translate what the teacher says in English into Japanese.*]

Whereas the emergent bilinguals (Satomi and Haruka) often translanguage because they were dependent on their expertise with other language practices in order to complete the task, the experienced bilinguals tend to *translanguage independently*. Yuji, for example, translanguages to enhance the task, demonstrating greater autonomy and ability to self-regulate his languaging. In all cases, however, both languages seem to be continuously activated, but to different degrees (Green, 1986; Thierry and Wu, 2007). The Japanese students interviewed in the García and Kano study revealed that all students, regardless of where they were positioned in the bilingual continuum, translanguaged frequently in order to make meaning and across purposes. They demonstrated much linguistic awareness of their own linguistic needs and were cognizant of their strengths and weaknesses. Beyond that, the students demonstrated

DOI: 10.1057/9781137385765

much autonomy and control in languaging appropriately for the task in which they were involved.

We now have much research evidence that students' translanguaging builds deeper thinking, provides students with more rigorous content, builds multiple subjectivities, and at the same time develops language and literacy practices that are adequate for specific academic tasks (Blackledge and Creese, 2010; Creese and Blackledge, 2010; Fitts, 2009; García, 2009a, 2013, 2014a,b, García, Flores and Woodley, 2012; Heller and Martin-Jones, 2001; Hornberger and Link, 2012; Lewis, Jones and Baker, 2012a,b; Li Wei, 2011b; Lin, 2013; Palmer and Martínez, 2013; Sayer, 2008, 2013). Whereas translanguaging for learners is a way to become more knowledgeable as language practices are expanded, for teachers, as we will see, it becomes a pedagogy to educate children holistically, but also to teach all the students in the classroom. And yet, as we will see, a translanguaging pedagogy that encompasses a multiplicity of signs and issues without privileging one over the other is almost impossible to construct in the schools of today. We focus in Chapter 6 on translanguaging as a pedagogy for teachers.

Notes

1   This study is reported at length in García, 2011c.
2   For more on this study, see García and Kano, forthcoming.

DOI: 10.1057/9781137385765

6

Translanguaging to Teach

Abstract: *In contrast to the pupil-directed translanguaging presented in Chapter 5, this chapter looks at translanguaging to teach, that is, at teacher-directed translanguaging, and its transformative potential. Translanguaging as pedagogy is contextualized through cases of how teachers with different characteristics use it in a variety of classrooms. The chapter considers how translanguaging involves co-learning by drawing on teacher–student interactions. Because translanguaging as pedagogy is transformative, the chapter pays attention to the development of sociocritical literacy among students, and to translanguaging as critical pedagogy for social justice. And because educational spaces outside of the structures of public schools are often more amenable to this critical lens, attention is paid in this chapter to the use of translanguaging in alternative educational spaces.*

Keywords: bilingual education; bilingualism; multiliteracies; teaching and bilingualism; transformative pedagogy; translanguaging

García, Ofelia, and Li Wei. *Translanguaging: Language, Bilingualism and Education.* Basingstoke: Palgrave Macmillan, 2014. DOI: 10.1057/9781137385765.

DOI: 10.1057/9781137385765

Teachers, pedagogies and translanguaging

Canagarajah (2011a) has pointed out that, 'we still have a long way to go in developing a taxonomy of translanguaging strategies and theorizing these practices' (415). He suggests then, that 'it is important that we develop our pedagogies ground up, from the practices we see multilingual students adopting' (415). This chapter starts to develop understandings of translanguaging as pedagogy from our observations of how students translanguage.

Given that translanguaging was originally coined in Welsh to teach bilingually, it has been Welsh scholars who have paid the most attention to its development as pedagogy. Williams (2012) sees translanguaging as a distinct pedagogic theory and practice that varies the language of input and output but with 'dual-language' processing for deeper learning.

Williams (2012) distinguishes between *natural translanguaging* and *official translanguaging*. *Natural translanguaging* refers mostly to acts by students to learn, described in the previous chapter, although it may also include the teachers' use of translanguaging with individuals, pairs and small groups 'to ensure full understanding of the subject material' (39). For example, in the following exchange, reported by Michael-Luna and Canagarajah (2007: 63), the teacher helps two students negotiate the meaning of 'warms', as in 'The sun warms the earth':

Teacher:	Do you know what warms means? What does warm mean? ... *¿No saben?* [You don't know?]
Students:	{Shake heads 'No'}
Teacher:	Oh, *ahora caigo*, now I understand. *Calentar* [to warm]
Student 1:	*Ooooh calentar*
Student 2:	*Calentar ... caras* [to warm ... faces]
Teacher:	So, *calienta su cara*. So it warms.... faces?
Student 2:	The land.
Student 1:	The land.

In contrast, *official translanguaging* is conducted and set up by the teacher. An official translanguaging pedagogy includes more planned actions of the teachers in interaction with students. Sometimes teachers adopt an official translanguaging pedagogy and translanguage to deepen explanations to the class of complex parts of the topic being taught or to have profound discussions of language or social issues. Other times, teachers

DOI: 10.1057/9781137385765

expect students to explain or write using their full language repertoire in order to show complete understanding of a subject area.

Lewis, Jones and Baker (2012b) differentiate between the pupil-directed translanguaging described in Chapter 5 and teacher-directed translanguaging. *Teacher-directed translanguaging* involves planned and structured activity by the teacher as a transformative pedagogy. In the diverse classrooms of today, learners have diverse profiles – not only linguistically, but also socially, educationally, experience-wise, and so on. For teachers, then, translanguaging is important not only because it allows them to engage each individual child holistically, but also because it is a way of differentiating instruction to ensure that all students are being cognitively, socially and creatively challenged, while receiving the appropriate linguistic input and producing the adequate linguistic output in meaningful interactions and collaborative dialogue.

Translanguaging as pedagogy refers to building on bilingual students' language practices flexibly in order to develop new understandings and new language practices, including those deemed 'academic standard' practices. A translanguaging pedagogy is important for language-minoritized students, whether they are emergent bilingual or not, because it builds on students' linguistic strengths. It also reduces the risk of alienation at school by incorporating languaging and cultural references familiar to language-minoritized students. Translanguaging as a pedagogical practice is increasingly being used not only to enable language-minoritized students to learn meaningfully, but also to sustain their dynamic languaging (Creese and Blackledge, 2010). In examining the translanguaging pedagogies used in complementary schools in the UK, Creese and Blackledge (2010) state:

> Both languages are needed simultaneously to convey the information, ... each language is used to convey a different informational message, but it is in the bilingualism of the text that the full message is conveyed. (108)

And in analyzing the pair work students do, they comment: 'It is the combination of both languages that keeps the task moving forward' (110).

Teachers use translanguaging strategically as a scaffolding approach to ensure that emergent bilinguals at the beginning points of the bilingual continuum engage with rigorous content, access difficult texts and produce new language practices and new knowledge. But translanguaging is also a *transformative pedagogy* capable of calling forth bilingual subjectivities and sustaining bilingual performances that go beyond

DOI: 10.1057/9781137385765

one or the other binary logic of two autonomous languages. As Henri Lefebvre, the French philosopher, points out, '*Il y a toujours l'Autre*', there is always an-Other term that disrupts categorical dichotomies, and a translanguaging pedagogy in its transformative phase attempts to do so, as it also changes ways of teaching and ways of learning. Translanguaging as pedagogy involves *leveraging,* that is, *deliberately* and simultaneously merging students' repertoires of practice, 'recruited as strengths' as Michaels (2005: 137) would say. This doesn't mean, however, that only teachers who are bilingual can engage in translanguaging pedagogies, as we will consider later (Flores and García, 2013). Contrary to what translanguaging requires of the learner who takes control of his or her language practices in order to access texts and knowledge, the teacher who uses translanguaging gives up her authority role in the classroom. Rather than teachers, they become facilitators, able to set up the project-based instruction and collaborative groupings that maximize translanguaging to learn. The teacher sets up the affordances for students to engage in discursive and semiotic practices that respond to their cognitive and social intentions. Translanguaging in teaching is always used in the service of providing rigorous instruction and maximizing interactions that would expand the students' language and meaning-making repertoire, including practices that fall under what some consider 'academic language'. Translanguaging has 'pedagogical value', since it is used 'both as part of [teachers'] linguistic toolkit for academic content learning and to valorize and promote pride in students' ethnolinguistic identities' (Sayer, 2008: 110). Nevertheless, teachers who adopt translanguaging as a pedagogy in today's schools often end up valuing it only as a way to ensure that students learn content and academic language. Part of our efforts as educators must be to ensure that we keep translanguaging from becoming just another strategy to deal with a problem.

Especially in contexts where higher-level texts are in a colonial or dominant language, a translanguaging pedagogy has been in effect for years, without much recognition in scholarship. For example, Lin (2013) has shown how, despite resistance from the state in Hong Kong, translanguaging pedagogies (or what she calls plurilingual pedagogies) are prevalent in teaching English. Mazak and her colleagues in CeIBA (Centro para la Investigación del Bilingüismo y el Aprendizaje) at the University of Puerto Rico in Mayagüez have focused on how a translanguaging pedagogy enables university educators to communicate appropriate

DOI: 10.1057/9781137385765

understandings to Spanish-speaking students who are not always fluent in the English of the classroom text. This is the case of the university science teacher described by Mazak and Herbas-Donoso (2013).

Adopting translanguaging to teach requires what Busch (2011) calls a 'critical gesture' of language practices that aims to develop a high degree of linguistic and social awareness. Following Busch (2011), one can say that teachers' translanguaging practices not only acknowledge the use of all students' language practices as a resource (what Bakhtin called *raznojazycie*), but in so doing also entail a commitment to multidiscursivity (what Bakhtin called *raznorecie*) that includes students' discourses, concerns, and topics of interest. But beyond this, a teacher who uses translanguaging as pedagogy participates as learner; that is, she adopts a multivoicedness, a *raznoglosie*, in Bakhtin's terms. We will return to this last role of the teacher in the section below on co-learning.

As we have said in Chapter 3, scholarship on bilingual education has focused on language allocation policies, as two or more languages are assigned to one structure or another (either time, content, person, place). These *macro-alternation policies* require attention, but are easily established. Teachers have to be taught to work within these structures efficiently, but the structure itself is easy to grasp. More difficult, however, is how to educate teachers to use translanguaging strategically *moment-by-moment* and as a *critical gesture*. This is the art of translanguaging as pedagogy, which we describe in the lessons of teachers in the next sub-section, before we summarize some principles of translanguaging as pedagogy.

Using translanguaging as pedagogy

Translanguaging as pedagogy can be used in different kinds of educational settings, and with different kinds of students. We describe in this section five different settings in which translanguaging as pedagogy is used by teachers in the United States.[1] Four of these cases are of different subject teachers in secondary schools – Math, Social Studies, Science and English Language Arts. One case is of a primary (elementary) school teacher of English as a Second Language. These teachers are on different points on the bilingual continuum, although they show a willingness to engage with translanguaging as pedagogy. In the secpedagogy enables university educators to communicate appropriate being language teachers. Because bilingualism in education in the US is usually limited to educating emergent bilinguals, most of our examples are in teaching those who are developing English. We find translanguaging a prevalent pedagogical practice in US secondary schools for immigrants with emergent bilinguals, and less so in elementary schools, except in some bilingual programs. But we have found translanguaging pedagogies across grades and types of programs. We also consider classrooms where translanguaging as pedagogy is being used to develop the pluriliteracy practices of students. We described in the prior section the reactions of students to the experimental curriculum set up by Kano; here we also describe the pedagogy that she used. We start first with emergent bilinguals in secondary schools, before considering an elementary classroom.

Translanguaging pedagogies for youth in secondary schools[2]

The number of recent immigrants entering US schools after the age of 15 has increased in the last decade. Thus, scholarly attention of bilingualism in schools is turning from elementary schools to secondary schools where the learning challenges are greater because the content taught is more difficult and there is less time to develop new language practices capable of expressing more sophisticated content. Translanguaging, as we will see, then serves as an important practice to teach these adolescents.

Teaching math

In one of the secondary schools for immigrant Latino newcomers, the Math teacher (who is bilingual) draws on the students' language practices in Spanish as she develops their English into a single bilingual repertoire.[3] The class follows a curriculum that the Math teachers in the school have adapted, and the worksheets are written in English, although they're annotated in Spanish and sometimes also have translations into Spanish. Following is the discourse that takes place during the first minutes of a lesson on perimeter:

> Teacher: OK, *¿quién quiere leer cuál es el* Do Now?[4]
> [Who wants to read the Do Now?]
> (Calls on a student who reads it in English)
> Teacher: *¿Quién más quiere leer?*
> [Who else wants to read?]
> (Calls on another student who reads it in English)

DOI: 10.1057/9781137385765

Teacher:	*Todos diciendo* …. (they all read chorally from the blackboard the Do Now, which is in English) [Everyone saying….]
Teacher:	*¿Quién quiere traducirlo en español?* [Who wants to translate it into Spanish?]
Student:	*¿Qué es la diferencia entre perímetro y área?* [What is the difference between perimeter and area?]
Teacher:	Repitan: What is the difference between perimeter and area? [Repeat]
Teacher:	*¿Cuál palabra es nueva para Uds. aquí?* [What word is new for you here?]
Students:	Perimeter (chorally).
Teacher:	*Así es*, perimeter, *perímetro*. [That's it].

In this brief exchange the Math teacher is speaking Spanish, although she has students read in English, repeat the written English on the blackboard, translate into Spanish and use their metalinguistic skills to identify new words. She finally repeats the term she is teaching in English and Spanish.

Another day, the Math teacher is teaching about correlations. Although she is teaching mostly through Spanish, she has the students write a sentence in their book in English. She points out the differences in pronoun use between English and Spanish:

> *En inglés no se omite el sujeto. Por favor, Ud. tiene que tener* 'he', 'she', 'it'.
> [In English you don't omit the subject. Please, you have to have 'he', 'she', 'it'].

And she then asks the class:

> *¿Quién me puede empezar esa oración en ingles? Vamos a ver, ¿quién me quiere empezar en inglés?*
> [Who can start that sentence in English? Let's see, who wants to start in English?]

At the end of class, after the students have understood the mathematical concept and have answered the worksheet in Spanish, she says:

> *Ahora tienen que elaborar una pequeña oración en inglés, una pequeña oracioncita en inglés. ¿Qué relación existe entre las calorías y los gramos de grasa? Por favor, una oracioncita pequeñita.*
> [Now you have to elaborate a small sentence in English, a little sentence in English. What relationship is there between calories and grams of fat? Please, a little sentence.]

DOI: 10.1057/9781137385765

At times during the lesson, the Math teacher provides terms in English for the concepts she is teaching in Spanish. She says, for example: '*Una línea recta, en inglés se dice* straight line'.

What this Math teacher stresses the most is that students could use their entire linguistic repertoire to demonstrate their mathematical knowledge; and yet, she is also building the students' ability to translanguage. No one is wrong, and no one way of saying anything is incorrect. During this lesson, she tells them:

> *Aquí nadie se equivoca. ¿Quién quiere decir algo?*
> [No one here is wrong. Who wants to say something?]

And when students do not speak up, she adds:

> *Uds. saben que pueden usar inglés,* spanglish *o español, ¿verdad que sí?*
> [You know that you can use English, Spanglish, or Spanish, right?].

This Math teacher knows that it is important for students to understand Mathematics, and that to do so, their entire cultural and linguistic repertoire has to be exploited through a translanguaging pedagogy. In so doing, she is developing in her students a sense of 'doing' bilingualism as US bilingual Latinos – leveraging their home language practices to develop school English literacy and sustaining their bilingualism at the same time by encouraging them to listen to, read and write Spanish, as well as English.

Teaching social studies

In another high school for immigrant Latino newcomers, Ms. Rojas teaches history to another group of Latino emergent bilinguals, using translanguaging in ways that develop students' sense of 'doing' bilingualism and also their critical consciousness to resist their stigmatization as racialized Others.[5] On the day of this lesson, Ms. Rojas explores legislation and policies surrounding race and interracial marriages in the history of the United States, a topic about which there are few resources in Spanish. She distributes an article in a teen publication that is in English. Groups of students read the text in English, and together they discuss the meaning of the text in Spanish and English. They annotate the English text with 'glosses', using words from Spanish. This is then followed by a whole class discussion that focuses on interracial marriage and race-based laws in the United States. As the students share their views, perspectives and questions in Spanish, they use English freely to

DOI: 10.1057/9781137385765

cite evidence from the English language text. To support their positions, they read aloud passages from the article in English.

The class then moves on to a writing exercise. The focusing question for the free writing exercise is in English: 'How big a role does race play in your life? How does it affect your views of yourself and your place in the world?' The teacher explains that this activity is 'about the content' and 'making connections', and it is thus important that students be allowed their full range of expression. The students' answers to this prompt are not only different in content, but also in the language of their response. For example, in examining three of the essays written by three girls, two of the girls' answers are written in Spanish, whereas another one is written in English. But the language choice has little to do with the content and intent, since the girls who wrote in Spanish talk about their lives in the United States, whereas the girl who writes in English, refers to Latin America. In Spanish, one of the girls talks about mixtures of races, including those that make up *'mi comunidad en los Estados Unidos'*, claiming and appropriating, in Spanish, her community in the United States. The other one who writes in Spanish shows metalinguistic awareness, pointing to the title/question that is written in English and providing a translation into Spanish – *'El título en sí está escrito en inglés, pero lo que significa en español es, Cuál es el gran rol que el español desempeña en nuestras vidas?'* But then, in Spanish, this student refers to *'la raza dominante'*, *'la blanca'* and to the racial prejudice that whites may show because *'suelen juzgar a los demás solo por el color de la piel'* ['they tend to judge others only by the color of their skin']. The student is expressing in Spanish, the racial prejudice she experiences in the US. In contrast, in the entry in English, the student not only refers to the student's 'country', her 'family' and her 'origins', but is written as the student 'went back to my country, my family and my origins'. It is through this going back that the student starts to question the historical reason for the racial mix – the enslavement of Africans and Asians to bring them to Latin America 'to make them work hard'. This student writes in English and questions issues of enslavement and inequities in her own life by going back to her roots, by interacting with a Latin American world to which she returns to make meaning of this deep question. Through English this Latina expresses the fact that people from Spain, Africa and Asia 'started to mix each other and in this way create new races'. It is precisely this sense of *mestizaje* that is creating this new Latino ethnolinguistic identity in the US, and new ways of performing language through translanguaging, that is, neither Spanish nor English, but 'new'. The translanguaging pedagogy

DOI: 10.1057/9781137385765

of the teacher creates a new reality because neither English nor Spanish is seen as static or dominant, but rather operates within a dynamic network of cultural and linguistic transformations. It is not two fixed identities or languages that are combined. Translanguaging opens up the space to talk about this dynamic relationship, and to actualize it in the classroom.

Teaching science

In a newcomer high school for Latino students that has a bilingual curriculum (Bartlett and García, 2011), the Science teacher uses a book written in English, as well as English-language material on earthquakes available online, as she teaches in 'Spanish'. An example of the classroom discourse follows.

Teacher:	Hit the bar. *Vamos con el foco. ¿Quién me puede leer lo que dice el foco, en inglés?* [Let's go to the focus. Who can read to me what the focus is in English?].
Student 1:	(Reads in English) Earthquakes are usually caused when rock underground suddenly breaks along a fault. The spot underground where the rock breaks is called the focus of the earthquake.
Teacher:	What does it say?
Student 2:	Focus is *foco ... y abajo*, underground, *cuando hay un break, allí es que ocurre el* earthquake. ...
Teacher:	The earthquake happens *cuando hay un* break underground. *Y qué es el* focus?
Student:	*El* focus *es dónde ocurre el* earthquake, *dónde está el* break, when rock break.

The bilingual teacher's pedagogical style, stressing the understanding of the scientific content and having students utilize their entire linguistic repertoire enables the students to integrate into their developing repertoire other language practices of school that some call 'English'.

Teaching English Language Arts[6]

In another school for newcomer immigrant Latino students, Camila Leiva is a teacher of English Language Arts (García, 2014b). But for Camila, education is about producing alternative knowledge that releases immigrant students' histories and discourses. To do so, she selects material carefully and uses a translanguaging pedagogy and discourse to critically situate her work. On this particular Monday, Camila is

DOI: 10.1057/9781137385765

working on the theme of literary conflicts. Camila starts by distributing a worksheet in which she reproduces part of the lyrics of the music video with space for students to translate from Spanish into English. Camila then plays the music video 'Sí se Puede' by El Chivo of Kinto Sol (www. myspace.com/video/kinto-sol/el-chivo-de-kinto-sol-quot-si-se-puede-quot-music-video-new/31015082) which communicates the idea that '*Yes, we can*' fight against deportation of undocumented immigrants and the separation of children who are US citizens from parents. The music video translanguages, starting with a white middle-aged man whose message is clear and in English: 'Illegals are invading our country & our government is doing nothing to stop them! Immigration is out of control, Fellows. We got to do something'. These words and images of the white man are interspersed with the words in 'Spanish' by the rapper with the refrain:

Por una causa y la misma razón	[For one cause and the same reason
Unidos todos sí se puede.	United we can.
Unidos todos con esta canción	United with this song,
Sí se puede.	Yes, we can.]

Also interspersed are images of children, all brown and clearly Latino, who are writing posters with counter-messages in both English and Spanish to the anti-immigrant message of the white man at the beginning:

'If you take my mother, it will hurt my heart.'
'Families need to be together.'
'*No me separen de mi mamá y mi papá.*' [Don't separate me from my mother and father.]

Also intermingled in the video are signs in English that reinforce the attitude of the white middle-aged man in the beginning – the bumper sticker on his jeep that reads 'America for Americans', the word 'criminal' on a sign, the deportation order for José Ramírez, the ICE (Immigration and Customs Enforcement) Police. The anti-immigrant messages are disrupted by the Latino children who are significantly wearing a T-shirt that says 'Born in the US'. The music video ends with one final image with a message written in English: '4 million US citizen children are fighting to keep their Moms and Dads'. Although in this analysis we're identifying the 'language' with which the lyrics are associated (and the teacher has done so also in the worksheet), the music video itself is translanguaged,

DOI: 10.1057/9781137385765

and from its perspective there isn't Spanish on one side and English on the other.

It is the translanguaging of the music video that creates a unity that is difficult to express, neither immigrant nor native and yet both; neither Spanish nor English, and yet a 'both' that is 'neither' because it is a new discourse, a product of post-coloniality, a translanguaging. Because the students and Camila are constituted in the translanguaging of the video, they are involved in a continuous becoming that is neither of one kind or another, but that constitutes the liberating action of the '*Sí se puede*'. As they follow the translanguaging, the students are confronted with alternative representations that release knowledge and voices that have been silenced by the dominant discourse about 'illegal' aliens in English that dominates the beginning of the video.

After playing the music video *Sí se Puede* twice, the students are asked to work in groups to provide a translation into 'English' of the portion rendered in 'Spanish' in the worksheet. Some students translate into English as best they can. Others, newly arrived the week before, simply copy the Spanish. Yet others write using both 'English', as well as 'Spanish' at times. All interact furiously, using dictionaries and iPads, asking questions of each other, leveraging their strengths in one language and the other, translanguaging collaboratively.

After giving the students opportunity to work together in their translations, there is a classroom dialogue in this supposedly 'English Language Arts' class which shows how and why both Camila and the students translanguage. The dialogue reproduced below makes up a two-minute segment of a longer dialogue (C stands for Camila, S for students; a number after S refers to different students):

1 C: Four million US citizens are being separated from their fathers and mothers because their parents are being deported.

2 S1: *Que los niños nacieron aquí. Legalmente son ciudadanos. Pero los padres no.*

3 S2: *Entonces esta es la preocupación de que los separen....*

4 C: It's a very worrying situation. So, because we don't have that much time and I want to get to the Eminem video.... What are four keywords? *Las palabras importantes, palabras claves?*

5 S3: *Deportar*

6 S4: Families together

7 S5: Protection

DOI: 10.1057/9781137385765

8   S6: Discrimination
9   C: I love how even though the song is in Spanish, we're choosing words in English. Kinto Sol grew up in the US but they do hip-hop in Spanish, and we're doing the same.
10   C: What problem do you see in the song?
11   S7: That many white people don't like Spanish people.
12   S8: It's the voice of the people.
13   C: The chivo, the rapper, says that some people don't like Latinos but ...
14   S1: *No sé cómo decirlo en inglés, pero ... . que los Latinos tenemos que pagar lo que otras personas ... .*
15   Ss: ... [inaudible].
16   C: Don't shoot her down. We're respecting each other's opinions. What else do we see?
17   S3: *Que las familias*, this guy, every time he has problem. Taking care something. It's a Latino that help. ...
18   C: The custodian is a Latino person. And who takes care of his daughter?
19   Ss: Latinos!
20   S2: *Miss, ¿yo puedo poner que muchas familias están separadas?*
21   C: *¿A causa de qué?*
22   S2: *Deportan los inmigrantes.*
23   C: How did you start the answer?
24   S2: They want the Latinos to get out of America.
25   C: What do you think the problem is? What is the type of conflict?
26   Ss: Me, me, me ... .
27   C: I like the enthusiasm. What type do you think it is?
28   S3: I have three. Because he has a problem with other people, and *cuando fueron reparar el carro; no es, pero que tiene un problema, pues así*, character vs. character.
29   C: What else can he say? Good ... new hands. People who haven't spoken.
30   S4: *Porque tiene un problema consigo mismo:* character vs. himself.
31   S5: *Porque los Latinos es una sociedad, y él es un character.*
32   C: Why do you think ...
33   S5: *que lo quieren matar?*
34   C: *Ramón, cuéntanos en español.*
35   C: Latinos, are we the majority or the minority?
36   Ss: Majority!/Minority!// *Somos mayoría en números!// No minoría!*

DOI: 10.1057/9781137385765

37 C: They call us a minority, even though we're a majority in many places. I'm going to give you some time before you finish. *Si ya terminaron, avancen a la segunda parte a la canción de Eminem..... .* (Observation, February 28, 2011).

Clearly the fact that Camila allows students to translanguage in the dialogue means that the voices of emergent bilinguals who otherwise would have been silenced are released and heard. The students' translanguaging serves three important discursive functions:

1   to participate,
2   to elaborate ideas,
3   to raise questions.

First, translanguaging allows all students to participate. In interaction 14, the student clearly states that he can't say it in English, and thus has to use Spanish. In interaction 17, another student uses Spanish to initiative participation, and find her voice. Second, translanguaging enables students to elaborate ideas, something they can't do in their limited voice in English only. For example, although the student in interaction 28 starts speaking in English, it is clear that if she's going to say more, she's going to have to use Spanish. Finally, students clearly understand that although the class is an English Language Arts class and the teacher is mostly using English, they can raise questions in Spanish, as the student in interaction 20 does.

But what is interesting in this dialogue is the way in which the teacher uses translanguaging. As with the students, translanguaging fulfills some discursive functions:

1   to involve and give voice,
2   to clarify,
3   to reinforce,
4   to manage the classroom, and
5   to extend and ask questions.

First, Camila translanguages to involve students, as when in interaction 34 she calls on Ramón to tell her what's going on in Spanish: 'Ramón, *cuéntanos en español*'. Second, Camila translanguages to clarify what she's been saying, as when in interaction 4 she asks the students to tell her 'the four keywords/*las palabras importantes/las palabras claves*'. Third, when students tell her in Spanish that the concern is that families would

DOI: 10.1057/9781137385765

be separated, she reinforces in English by saying: 'It's a very worrying situation' (interaction 4). Fourth, she uses translanguaging for classroom management, for example, when in interaction 37, she turns to Spanish to tell students to hurry up, '*avancen a la segunda parte…*'. Finally, Camila translanguages to go beyond the lesson, to extend it, to pose questions, as when in interaction 21, she turns to Spanish to clearly pose a Why question, '*A causa ¿de qué?*' Camila uses language flexibly to enable students to learn, to develop academic concepts and language, to think critically and to act on the world.

But beyond the important discursive functions that translanguaging fulfills, translanguaging, as 'an-other tongue' as Mignolo would say, clearly opens up an in-between space where alternative representations are released. When a student starts saying something and the rest of the class yells at her, Camila firmly tells them: 'Don't shoot her down. We're respecting each other's opinions' (interaction 26). Translanguaging opens up a space of tolerance and respect that goes beyond the illegality and criminality that is transmitted by the white middle-aged man in the beginning.

This space of tolerance is not a static space, but a new emerging and dynamic space where sociocultural transformations are possible. For example, through translanguaging Camila is helping students construct a Latino pan-ethnicity. The Latino immigrants in this school are from many different national backgrounds. In the US they come together for the first time, bringing their different histories, geographies, cultures, language features. It is not enough simply to construct English fluency. For this US Latino population to succeed, it is important to also construct a Latino pan-ethnicity. Camila clearly points this out when she says in interaction 31, '*Los Latinos es una sociedad.*' It is significant that she says '*es*'; not 'we are', nor 'they are', but 'is a society', a new space of possibilities, neither we, nor they. Translanguaging makes it evident that we cannot separate our languaging from the way in which we perceive the world, but it also makes it possible to assume an in-between position that resists the asymmetries of power instilled by standard language practices in school.

Camila is not constructing a closed Latino pan-ethnicity, but one where fluid identities are being brought forth with others in a process of continuous becoming. In interaction 9, she says: 'Even though the song is in Spanish, we're choosing words in English. Kinto Sol grew up in the US, but they do hip-hop in Spanish, and we're doing the same.'

DOI: 10.1057/9781137385765

Camila wants to create through translanguaging a discourse that goes beyond autonomous languages that represent sole national or transnational identities. Rather, translanguaging for her opens up possibilities of participation, while generating the fluid subjectivities that Latinos need to succeed in US society. Translanguaging gives back the voice that had been taken away by ideologies of monoglot standards (Silverstein, 1996), whether of English or Spanish. The US Latino 'languagelessness' (Rosa, 2010) is converted into voice. In this 'English' classroom for Latino immigrants, translanguaging releases students from the constraints of both an Anglophone ideology that demands English monolingualism for US citizens, and a Hispanophone ideology that blames US Latinos for speaking 'Spanglish' (Otheguy and Stern, 2010; Zentella, 1997). But translanguaging as pedagogy has not been taken up only in secondary schools. The teacher in the next section teaches primary school in a self-contained English as a Second Language classroom. Regardless of the program designation, the teacher is most effective in taking up translanguaging as pedagogy.

Translanguaging pedagogies in an ESL primary classroom[7]

Christina Celic teaches an elementary school classroom for third and fourth graders (8- and 9-year-olds) who are all emergent bilinguals, some who are recent immigrants, others who were born in the US. The school has only an English as a Second Language program, and thus, classroom instruction is supposed to be in English only. Although most children in Christina's class are from Latin America and speak Spanish, there are also four Chinese speakers and a Nepalese-speaking child. Christina is not of Spanish-speaking descent, but is bilingual.

Christina, a master teacher (see her own masterful description of appropriate practices in Celic, 2009), uses a balanced-literacy workshop approach to the teaching of English reading and writing. For her mini-lessons, she calls students to the rug in the front of the room. Sometimes during the mini-lesson Christina reads a book out loud; other times, she teaches an explicit language or literacy function or form. The children sit in duos and trios on the floor, grouped according to home language but heterogeneously by English language ability. That is, children who have more English proficiency are paired with those who have less. Christina scaffolds the mini-lesson by modeling intensely and then providing the children with an opportunity to discuss what she has explicitly taught

DOI: 10.1057/9781137385765

or read. To do that, she asks the children to 'turn and talk' to their partner(s) and to discuss (or repeat) what she has modeled. But not all the children can make sense of what Christina has taught. Some have understood it fully and can produce it; others, not so much. Thus, the groups of children work in and out of 'English', offering explanations in 'Spanish' in some groups, in 'Chinese' in others. The Nepalese child often pairs up with Christina who offers pictures, drawings and acting out to contextualize the task.

When the children go back to their desks to read and write, they continue to work in collaborative groups, but this time in larger groups of about six students with a common home language who are more homogeneous in English literacy. That is, children reading in more or less the same level of English work together, reading the same text, interrogating each other, discussing ideas. Although the children read in English, they translanguage as they discuss the texts. Every day Christina works with a different reading group in guided reading, providing first an introduction and orientation to the text, and presenting key vocabulary. When working with Spanish-speaking groups of very low English proficiency, Christina listens to them read in English, often having them first repeat. She frequently asks students for translations or does so herself. Finally, children are encouraged to translanguage during the discussion as they try out their ideas with new language practices.

Although Christina cannot provide bilingual guided reading to the Chinese-speaking group, she does encourage translanguaging among them, as they discuss the text and pose and answer questions of each other. Often the children write translations to key vocabulary in word walls in Chinese. And the Chinese children, as well as all the children, including the Nepalese child, have dictionaries and iPads that they consult often.

It is in independent reading when the children have the most opportunities to work through their own languaging. Christina provides children with zip-lock bags that hold authentic children's books in English, as well as books in Spanish, Chinese and Nepalese at their own grade level. Even though the children's books in Spanish have been leveled by New York City's Department of Education, the same cannot be said of books in Chinese and Nepalese. For that, Christina has involved the Chinese and Nepalese parents, as well as the community.

In writing, Christina allows students to write essays in Spanish, Chinese or Nepalese. Although she can read the students' writing in Spanish, she often asks students to provide her with an oral summary

DOI: 10.1057/9781137385765

of what the essay says in English or she has one of the other students do so. She also points out to the children how expert literary texts are often bilingual and together they explore the effect of writing bilingually. By allowing the children to develop a languaging voice as authors regardless of official classroom language, and to translanguage, the children become authors very quickly, eventually able to write essays in standard English when prompted to do so.

An example of this development is the case of a child whom we will call Rosa. In September, the first month of school in the US, Rosa could only write patterns of 'I see' in English together with drawing a picture. She writes: 'I see a teacher'; I see a student'; 'I see a clock'. And she accompanies these sentences and the many that follow with a picture which she draws for each item. At the same time, however, in September, Rosa could also write a full essay in Spanish. It is important to note that the child starts out by describing *'Era una noche que llegé (sic) conocí a mi familia'* ['It was the first night I arrived, I met my family.'] Because Christina allowed her to write in Spanish, Rosa not only demonstrated her expertise in writing, but also her experience in meeting her family for the first time. It turns out that this child, as many others, had been raised by her grandmother after her mother left for the US to work. In the US she remarried and had children. This child was meeting now, for the first time, her siblings and step-father. Because she was given permission to write in her home language, she revealed important information about herself which the teacher would have never known if she had been restricted to writing in English only. By allowing the student to develop her voice in writing, regardless of language practices, by November, two months after the child arrived in school, Rosa wrote an essay about the topic of the Unit that they had been working on – Native Americans. In that essay she starts out by writing the topic sentence in English: 'Many years ago, there was a group of Native Americans called the Iroquois.' And she continues in Spanish: *'Los Iroquois utilizaban muchos animales ...'*. As she develops her essay in Spanish, Rosa incorporates into her writing the English content words that she has appropriated:

> *El* fish hook *es un anzuelo para los peces. ... También hay un* war club *es como un martillo, mas parece una roca ... También hay un* spoon *es una cuchara con ella comen.*

Rosa not only used 'fish hook', 'war club', 'spoon' in English; she shows that she also knows the words in Spanish. By February, five months

DOI: 10.1057/9781137385765

after her arrival, this child was able to write an essay in English with help from the teacher, something she would never have accomplished if the teacher had only allowed her to write in the simplified English she knew in September. By developing a voice through translanguaging, this child was able to extend her written repertoire to encompass standard English.

Christina's classroom is in principle in 'English' only. However, the multilingual realities of the classroom are performed in translanguaging ways every day, as children are encouraged to make sense of what is being communicated and taught. In the next section, we consider how a translanguaging pedagogy has also been found to be highly effective in teaching literacy in different contexts.

Translanguaging pedagogies for pluriliteracies

Paying attention to the teaching of writing in a dual language bilingual first-grade classroom, Michael-Luna and Canagarajah (2007) identified translanguaging pedagogical strategies, which they refer to as codemeshing strategies. These strategies included selecting multilingual texts, that is, including texts in different languages and with different semiotic resources, so as to active prior knowledge. Translanguaging strategies also included modeling oral and written codemeshing so as to encourage student agency in language choice. Finally, translanguaging strategies were also used by the teacher to scaffold the negotiation with the text.

In the Canadian Multiliteracies Project, teachers developed a variety of multilingual multimodal identity-texts (Cummins and Early, 2011; Schechter and Cummins, 2003). Students used their families' multilingualism as a resource, and were engaged in translanguaging exercises, supported by the teacher. The multilingual and translanguaged identity-texts produced by the students reflected and transformed their subjectivities. Through their engagement with translanguaged writing students were able to recognize the ways in which texts are inscribed by ideology, as well as the ways in which they assume identities and become subjects.

In reading, the students' home languages have been identified as an important resource. Moll et al. (1992) showed that when Latino students were able to discuss English texts in Spanish, they comprehended much more than when they were limited to English only. Martínez-Roldán and Sayer (2006) also demonstrated how the Latino students' use of their bilingual vernacular, what they called 'Spanglish', was a powerful

DOI: 10.1057/9781137385765

intellectual tool that allowed them to mediate the standard language used in academic reading texts.

Teacher practices of supporting students in identifying cognates has also been shown to result in enriched meaning-making in reading in both English and Spanish (Jiménez, García and Pearson, 1995; Langer et al., 1990). Teaching what cognates are and how they work across languages is also a strategy promoted by Escamilla and colleagues (2013). Other strategies to develop metalanguage and make cross-language connections identified by Escamilla and colleagues are the use of bilingual books, strategic use of language, as well as a technique they call *Así se dice (That's how you say it)*. In *Así se dice*, teachers encourage students to collaboratively interpret and translate a chosen text and discuss the translation. Escamilla and her colleagues also list preview-review and anchor charts as examples of strategic use of bilingual languaging. *Preview-review* is a strategy that is frequently used in bilingual classrooms, where the teacher uses the students' home language to activate prior knowledge and summarize key concepts, and then teaches the lesson mostly through the other language of instruction. Students then can summarize and synthesize their new learning in their home language. *Anchor charts* are co-created by teachers and students and provide explicit comparisons of language features. Although all the teacher lessons reported up to now have taken place in regular government-funded schools, the case below describes an experimental curriculum, delivered not in a traditional school program but as a private class that focused on translanguaging as pedagogy.

Pluriliteracies for Japanese American students

The translanguaging pedagogy used in the experimental curriculum developed by Naomi Kano (2010) (her students' translanguaging was described in Chapter 5) enabled Japanese students to become more aware of the differences in the construction of Japanese and English written texts, so that they would be able to produce better English essays. Her translanguaging pedagogy followed three steps, going between the use of one language or the other, as defined in school:

1 Students read bilingual texts on the topic about which they were assigned to write. These bilingual texts were presented side-by-side, or there was an English text coupled with a parallel translation in Japanese, or a set of English and Japanese texts about the same subject, but not parallel translations.

DOI: 10.1057/9781137385765

2   Students discussed the bilingual readings mostly in Japanese.
3   Students wrote an essay in English on the topic of the bilingual reading and the discussion in Japanese about the readings.

As reported by García and Kano (forthcoming), a translanguaging pedagogy which took into account the entire linguistic and discursive repertoire of Japanese students produced better written texts in one language, English. And although this was not the purpose of the study, in some cases evidence was provided through interviews that students' greater awareness of language differences as a result of translanguaging also had repercussions in their understanding and construction of Japanese written texts. The translanguaging pedagogy, enabling students to move back and forth along their entire linguistic repertoire actually overcame the differences in language, discourse and idea inventory of Japanese American students writing in English. That is, their English essay repertoire was enriched through the inclusion and attention paid to the students' Japanese languaging and cultural practices, including their entire semiotic repertoire. But for all teachers to adapt a translanguaging curriculum or use translanguaging pedagogies as Kano did in this case, all teachers need to be learners, to co-learn, as another section makes clear. Translanguaging can also be done by monolingual teachers, as shown in the next section.

Monolingual teachers using translanguaging

Although teachers in the examples above had different degrees of bilingual proficiency, translanguaging can also be successfully used by monolingual teachers or teachers who do not share the languages of their students. For example, in the schools of the International Network for Public High Schools in New York City for recently arrived immigrants, all teachers use translanguaging to educate their highly linguistically diverse student body. Since it would be impossible to speak all the students' languages, teachers group students in homogeneous home language groups so that students could assist each other in making meaning of the lesson.

García, Flores and Woodley (2012) have documented how teachers with different language proficiencies working in two secondary New York City schools with a large number of Latino emergent bilinguals

DOI: 10.1057/9781137385765

use translanguaging as pedagogy. Three pedagogical metafunctions for translanguaging are identified as used by all teachers in the study: (1) the contextualization of key words and concepts, (2) the development of metalinguistic awareness and (3) the creation of affective bonds with students.

In a school for Latino recently arrived immigrants, Flores and García (2013) have documented the work of a teacher of Indian background who speaks five languages, even though Spanish is not one of them.[8] In interacting with her Spanish-speaking students, she has acquired some vocabulary and phrases in Spanish. She translates key terms of the day into Spanish to scaffold instruction and build on students' prior knowledge. She does so by asking another student for the term or using Google Translate. The following exchange, taken from a day in which she was asking students to write an essay using comparisons, is typical in this teacher's classroom:

Teacher: To write a comparison between Julio and myself. Can someone
say it in Spanish?
Student: *Que tiene que comparar ellos.*
Student: *Algo que ellos tienen en común.*

The teacher recognizes what the students know and asks for their help in translating for others, in that way making it comprehensible for all. The teacher continues:

Teacher: What is different? *Diferente?*
Student: Different? *Tamaño.*
Teacher: *Tamaño.* Size.
Student: Your skin, different color.

The fact that this teacher risked saying words in Spanish means that students can also risk saying more in English. She repeats their words in Spanish (*tamaño*), in the same way the students repeat her words in English (*different*). And this trust and open exchange of different language practices enable students to bring up the difficult topic of skin color and racial differences.

Flores and García (2013) describe the way in which this teacher used translanguaging to handle an incident that occurred during a public presentation by a Spanish-speaking student:

After being pressured by other teachers to present in English, a student completely shut down and refused to speak. [The teacher] started to

DOI: 10.1057/9781137385765

communicate with the student through a translator, but ended up having a direct conversation with the student utilizing translanguaging strategies. Her message was completely understood, as she expressed the importance of taking risks languaging. In so doing, she became a model of the very experimentation that she was encouraging in the student. It is one thing for a monolingual teacher to encourage students to take risks, and quite another for a teacher to model what taking these risks might look like.

The teacher makes an effort to make herself understood using Spanish, and the students try to make themselves understood using English. In so doing, more English is being added to the linguistic repertoire of the students, and more Spanish to that of the teacher.

This example makes evident that teachers do not need to be bilingual in order to take up translanguaging to educate. Many monolingual teachers encourage and set up translanguaging spaces in their classrooms where bilingual students can use all their language resources. There are also many monolingual teachers, like the one portrayed above, who try out translanguaging with their students. The advantage, of course, is that it shows students how to privilege interaction and collaborative dialogue over form, and thus develops their voice.

Translanguaging as co-learning

Using the complementary schools for British Chinese children in several cities in England, Li Wei (2014) examined how translanguaging is used not only by pupils and teachers as learning or teaching strategies separately, but also together in a process he calls 'co-learning', where multiple agents simultaneously try to adapt to one another's behavior so as to produce desirable outcomes that would be shared by the contributing agents. Co-learning in the classroom does not simply involve the teacher in developing strategies to allow equitable participation for all in the classroom; co-learning requires much unlearning of cultural conditioning because, as Brantmeier (online) points out, 'it challenges the traditional authoritative, dominant and subordinate role sets in schooling environments and the unequal power relationships in wider spheres of our world'. It empowers the learner, and 'builds a more genuine community of practice'. It moves the teacher and the learner toward a more 'dynamic and participatory engagement' in knowledge construction. According to Brantmeier, the characteristics of a co-learning relationship include:

DOI: 10.1057/9781137385765

▸ All knowledge is valued
▸ Reciprocal value of knowledge sharers
▸ Care for each other as people and co-learners
▸ Trust
▸ Learning from one another

And the characteristic of a co-learning classroom environment, according to Brantmeier, are:

▸ Shared power among co-learners
▸ Social and individualized learning
▸ Collective and individual meaning-making and identity exploration
▸ Community of practice with situated learning
▸ Real-world engagement and action

The following example was recorded in a Mandarin class in a Cantonese school in London. The teacher has written the Chinese characters for a particular type of cookie, 曲奇, on the white board because she thought it was an unfamiliar word for the pupils. As it happens, the word is a Cantonese transliteration of English and some of the pupils recognize the characters, as they have seen them in local shops. The Cantonese pronunciation of the characters is *kuk-kei*, as G2 (Girl 2), one of the pupils, says in Example 1. But the teacher, not knowing Cantonese, pronounces the word in Mandarin, which sounds very different from the English source, *cookie*. The two pupils explain to the teacher that the Cantonese pronunciation of the characters is in fact very similar to the English word. What is particularly remarkable is that when the teacher seeks confirmation (*Is it?*), G2 replies in Cantonese, *haila*, meaning yes, reinforcing the fact they are Cantonese speakers. So while the pupils are learning Mandarin, their knowledge of Cantonese helps with the proceeding of the class, while the teacher gains knowledge about the origin of the Chinese word by learning from the pupils.

Example 1

(T: Female teacher; G1 and G2 are two female pupils, 11 years old.)

T: 曲奇(quqi). 一种饼干, 知道吗?
      Quqi. A kind of cookie, you know?
G1:   What?
T: 曲奇(quqi).
G2:   *kuk-kei. kuk-kei.*
T: Yes.

DOI: 10.1057/9781137385765

G1:   So why did you say *qiu* … something *qiu* …

T: 曲奇(ququi).

G2:   No. *kuk-kei.*

G1:   广东话是 *kuk-kei.*
     In Cantonese it is kuk-kei.

G2:   It's Cantonese. *kuk-kei* is Cantonese.

T: 是吗?
     Is it?

G2:   係啦!
     Yes.

Many comparable instances were observed in Li Wei's fieldwork in the Chinese complementary schools in Britain where the pupils' knowledge of Cantonese has proved to be particularly useful in the teaching and learning of specific words and phrases, many of which are transliterations of English. Examples include 沙律 *salad*, in Cantonese *saaleot* and in Mandarin 色拉 *sela*; 芝士 *cheese*, in Cantonese *zisi* and Mandarin *zhishi*. The Mandarin teachers, while assuming an influential status in the class and teaching what is assumed to be a high-status variety of Chinese, gains by learning from the pupils.

Another example was recorded in the Mandarin school in London, in which the teacher is explaining the text 送爷爷回家 meaning *taking granddad home*. But her English translation 'took grandfather to the home' does not only sound bookish, but is also pragmatically misleading. Chinese learners of English often have problems with the use of articles in English. The teacher evidently does not know the difference between *home*, which can be used as an adverb, and *the home*. This causes one of the pupils to remark on the Chinese tradition of looking after the elderly within their own families rather than sending them to care centers. What is interesting in Example 2 is that, while the boy (B) realizes that he misunderstood the teacher because of the way she phrased it, the teacher does not seem to realize that the word *home* can also refer to care centers for the elderly.

Example 2

(T: Female teacher. B: Boy, 12 years old.)

T: (Reading the textbook) 送爷爷回家, took grandfather to the home.
                            [send granddad home]

B: Aren't the Chinese supposed to be nice to their grandparents?

T: Yes, of course.

B: Why is she sending him to a home then?

DOI: 10.1057/9781137385765

T: What?

B: You said she sent the granddad to a home.

T: 对，家 home. 回家 going home.

B: Not an old people's home then.

T: What?

B: Doesn't matter.

In this case, the teacher wasted an opportunity to learn from her students. This example also illustrates the discrepancies in the cultural knowledge that exist between the teachers and the pupils. Many of the teachers have only been in Britain for a short period of time. The pupils, on the other hand, are mostly British-born. They have relatively little in common in terms of cultural background and life experience. This lack of commonality between the teachers and the pupils can potentially cause difficulties in the classroom and beyond, unless they engage actively in co-learning.

Translanguaging for sociocritical literacy

Beyond the inclusion of different language practices, translanguaging opens up a space of resistance and social justice, since language practices of minoritized youth are usually racialized and stigmatized (Rosa, 2010). Gutiérrez (2008) reports on how instructors in a summer program for youth from migrant farmworker backgrounds privileged 'hybrid language practices' to 'incite, support, and extend students' repertoires of practice' (160), what she calls their *sociocritical literacy*. Translanguaging as pedagogy requires a sociocritical approach to teaching. This is precisely the position of the high school teacher, Camila Leiva, described above. By exposing alternative histories, representations and knowledge, translanguaging has the potential to crack the 'standard language' bubble in education that continues to ostracize many bilingual students, and most especially immigrants, indigenous peoples and other minoritized students.

Because this sociocritical positioning is often not allowed in classrooms in state schools, studies of translanguaging as pedagogy are increasingly situated in informal educational settings, and especially in after-school or supplementary programs like the one portrayed earlier. Blackledge and Creese (2010) studied the flexible bilingualism present in eight complementary schools in four UK cities, and for four linguistic

DOI: 10.1057/9781137385765

communities. Creese and Blackledge (2010) identified the following pedagogical strategies to promote 'flexible bilingualism':

1   Use of bilingual label quests, repetition and translation across languages.
2   Ability to engage audiences through translanguaging and heteroglossia.
3   Use of student translanguaging to establish identity positions both oppositional and encompassing of institutional values.
4   Recognition that languages do not fit into clear bounded entities and that all languages are 'needed' for meanings to be conveyed and negotiated.
5   Endorsement of simultaneous literacies and languages to keep the pedagogic task moving.
6   Recognition that teachers and students skillfully use their languages for different functional goals such as narration and explanation.
7   Use of translanguaging for annotating texts, providing greater access to the curriculum, and lesson accomplishment. (112–113)

The chapters in García, Zakharia and Otcu (2013) address the translanguaging pedagogies used by teachers in different bilingual community programs in the city of New York to teach the increasingly diverse students who attend these programs. In fact, the teachers in all of the cases in the book discuss how they routinely violate school-wide policies that insist that only the community language be used. This has to do with the fact that community language use precisely consists of translanguaging. A Persian-speaking parent explains:

> I habitually love and praise my children in Persian, and habitually send them to bed and tell them to brush their teeth in English. ... The notion of ethnic language is false; we don't teach Persian to our children as part of their heritage or identity, and tell them that's why they have to learn it, because that ethnicizes Persian; that provincializes Persians... They will work here, have friends here; they are Americans, they need to speak English. (Shirazi and Borjian, 2013: 166)

Community language use in bilingual contexts is dynamic and consists of translanguaging practices that work to transform the subjectivities and consciousness of students. Because of its grounding in social theory, translanguaging connects to the linguistic human rights agenda (Skutnabb-Kangas, 2000) by giving voice to those who language differently.

DOI: 10.1057/9781137385765

Translanguaging is the norm used to teach and learn in communities, extending participants' sociocritical literacy. For example, in another innovative after-school program, Gutiérrez, Bien, Selland and Pierce (2011) leverage translanguaging as a pedagogical resource (although they refer to it as hybridity), as they challenge the divide between 'everyday and school-based literacies' (258). Also, Pahl (2004) has studied children's translanguaging in homes, as they produce multimodal/ multilingual texts where drawings, photographs, oral and written narratives are interwoven in narratives that span various time frames and geographical spaces, thus constructing their multiple identities. Finally, Sánchez (2007) focused on how artifacts, both real or pictorial, generated immigrant students' narratives of transnational experiences, as they drew on different language and literacy practices for the presentation of self in co-authoring a bilingual (Spanish–English) children's picture book documenting their cross-border (US–Mexico) experience. All of these cases give evidence of how it is especially in alternative educational spaces that translanguaging as pedagogy often fulfills its promise to truly open up spaces for meaning-making and social justice.

Examples such as these, and the examples we discussed in the earlier sections, have important implications for education and teacher education. In the last chapter we start by summarizing the principles and strategies of translanguaging for teaching and learning that we have developed in Chapters 5 and 6. We also address the importance of teacher education and discuss a project which uses translanguaging as its cornerstone. We end the chapter by addressing two important remaining challenges for translanguaging – the reluctance of teaching students to actually do translanguaging in state schools, as well as the reluctance of using translanguaging in assessment.

Notes

1   Some of the lessons of the teachers that are presented here have been the object of studies by García and colleagues and have appeared or will appear in other papers. They are brought together here. We identify in the text where these cases have appeared elsewhere.

2   The teachers in this section have been profiled in the following: the teacher of Math and the teacher of social studies in García, Flores and Woodley (forthcoming). The Science teacher is portrayed in Bartlett and García, 2011.

DOI: 10.1057/9781137385765

Finally, the English Language Arts teacher's lesson is described in García, 2014b.

3 This teacher was part of a study of Pan American High Schools conducted by García and Flores.

4 In New York City schools, teachers are required to have on the blackboard a 'Do Now', which is a short activity that students must do when they first come into a class, after they change teachers and subjects. It is meant to get students to settle down, take out their notebooks and pencils and focus on the new content.

5 This lesson was observed as part of the Latinos in New York City High School studies.

6 An expanded version of this lesson appears in García, 2014b.

7 This teacher has been portrayed in García, 2013b.

8 This lesson has been described in Flores and García, 2013.

DOI: 10.1057/9781137385765

7

Translanguaging in Education: Principles, Implications and Challenges

▶

Abstract: *In some ways this chapter summarizes and contextualizes the chapters in Part II, and presents important challenges to translanguaging in education. The chapter starts by presenting Principles and Strategies for translanguaging as pedagogy. Because teacher education would be so important for the acceptance of translanguaging in classrooms, the chapter both discusses teacher education in general and describes in more detail a particular project to work with school leaders and teachers where translanguaging is the cornerstone of the shifts required in schools. Finally, the chapter ends with what we see to be the two most important challenges for adoption of a theory of translanguaging in education – the reluctance to develop students' understandings of how to do translanguaging, and the development of translanguaged assessments.*

Keywords: assessment; bilingualism; teacher education; translanguaging

García, Ofelia, and Li Wei. *Translanguaging: Language, Bilingualism and Education.* Basingstoke: Palgrave Macmillan, 2014. DOI: 10.1057/9781137385765.

Translanguaging as pedagogy: principles and strategies

As we have seen, despite much monolingual instruction and language separation in language education programs, teachers use translanguaging to enable students to make meaning and learn. It is in the creative and critical moments of translanguaging that actions are transformed. This leads to substantive teaching and learning, as well as transformations.

Table 7.1 summarizes the different ways in which translanguaging is used by teachers in schools to ensure that bilingual students learn both content and language.

As seen in Table 7.1, column 1, translanguaging is used by teachers for seven different goals:

TABLE 7.1   *Teaching to learn content and language through translanguaging*

Why? GOAL	What? POSSIBLE STRATEGIES
1 Differentiate and adapt	Translation
2 Build background knowledge	Collaborative dialogue Collaborative grouping Reading multilingual texts Multilingual listening/Visual resources Project learning Thematic units Research
3 Deepen understanding, develop and extend new knowledge, critical thinking	All of the above + Inner speech Multilingual writing
4 Cross-linguistic transfer and metalinguistic awareness	Word walls Sentence starters Cognates Comparing multilingual texts Multilingual vocabulary inquiry Multilingual syntax/Morphology inquiry
5 Cross-linguistic flexibility	Alternating languages and media Translating Translanguaging in writing Translanguaging in speaking
6 Identity investment and positionality	All of the above
7 Interrogate linguistic inequality	All of the above

DOI: 10.1057/9781137385765

1   To *differentiate among students'* levels and adapt instruction to different types of students in multilingual classrooms; for example, those who are bilingual, those who are monolingual and those who are emergent bilinguals.

2   To *build background knowledge* so that students can make meaning of the content being taught and of the ways of languaging in the lesson.

3   To *deepen understandings and sociopolitical engagement*, develop and extend new knowledge, and develop critical thinking and critical consciousness.

4   For *cross-linguistic metalinguistic awareness* so as to strengthen the students' ability to meet the communicative exigencies of the socioeducational situation.

5   For *cross-linguistic flexibility* so as to use language practices competently.

6   For *identity investment and positionality*; that is, to engage learners.

7   To *interrogate linguistic inequality and disrupt linguistic hierarchies and social structures.*

Repeating the definition by García and Kano (forthcoming) cited in Chapter 4, translanguaging is 'a process by which students and teachers engage in complex discursive practices that include ALL the language practices of ALL students in a class in order to develop new language practices and sustain old ones, communicate and appropriate knowledge, and give voice to new sociopolitical realities by interrogating linguistic inequality.' The definition reflects the goals outlined in Table 7.1. Goals 1, 2 and 3 relate to communicating and appropriating knowledge; goals 4 and 5 to developing new language practices and sustaining old ones; and goals 6 and 7 to giving voice and shaping new sociopolitical realities by interrogating linguistic inequality.

The goals of a translanguaging pedagogy are accompanied by translanguaging strategies (see Table 7.1, second column) that can be carried out either in general education (monolingual education) or bilingual education. The translanguaging strategies identified in Table 7.1 correspond to three categories:

1   Teacher attentiveness to meaning-making, by:
    ▶ Translanguaging when appropriate for understanding.
    ▶ Encouraging students' translanguaging in inner speech.

2   Teacher use and design of classroom resources for translanguaging, which include:
    ▶ The availability and production of multilingual and multimodal texts, including fiction, informational texts and reference resources.

DOI: 10.1057/9781137385765

▸ The availability and production of technologically enhanced media, including iPads and computers.

▸ The availability and production of a multilingual/multimodal classroom landscape that includes, among others, listening and visual centers and texts, technologically enhanced media, multilingual word walls, multilingual sentence starters and cognate walls.

3   Teacher design of curriculum and classroom structures for translanguaging, which include:

▸ Peer grouping according to home language, to enable collaborative dialogue and cooperative tasks using translanguaging.

▸ Project- and task-based learning, to build on multimedia and kinesthetics.

▸ Research tasks, so that students can translanguage, as they find new information.

▸ Curriculum thematic units, to integrate ways of languaging and producing knowledge.

▸ Language-inquiry tasks, for example cross-linguistic comparisons that include cognate-identification, to build translanguaging capacities and extend metalinguistic awareness.

It is beyond the scope of this short book to expand on these strategies, but the reader will find an excellent resource in Celic and Seltzer (2012) and in García, Ibarra-Johnson and Seltzer (forthcoming).

Implications of translanguaging for teacher education

All teachers in the 21st century need to be prepared to be bilingual teachers (Adelman, Reyes and Kleyn, 2010; García, 2009a); that is, they need to see themselves as building on and developing the students' additional languages while educating them. But in most teacher education institutions throughout the world, the students' multilingualism is an after-thought, and teachers learn little about the children's complex and dynamic language practices.

In an article on teacher education for multilingual education, García and Kleyn (2013) identify the development of the teachers' understandings of bilingual students and their families, as being most important. All teachers need to be able to observe bilingual children closely and describe them as they are engaged in meaningful learning activities and interacting in different settings. Teachers need, in other words, to be aware of language diversity and to see their students as people, not just numbers (see Hélot and Young, 2006, for a description of a *language awareness program* in Alsace). But beyond linguistic and cultural information, teachers need to develop a critical sociopolitical consciousness about the linguistic diversity of the children and, in the case of bilingual teachers, the historical glottopolitics of the languages they're trying to develop. Teachers then need to act on all this information by constructing curricula and pedagogies that build on the sociopolitical, sociohistorical and sociolinguistic profiles of the bilingual children in question.

Daria Witt, Director of Professional Development Services for the International Network of Public High Schools described by García and Sylvan (2011), is developing, along with her staff and teachers, activities

Directions: *Take the cards that are in your envelopes and work in a pair or triad to sort them into examples of translanguaging and non-examples of translanguaging. Keep in mind the following characteristics of translanguaging (from a teacher perspective) covered during the presentation:*

- Students are allowed to use their entire linguistic repertoire to make meaning in the classroom

- Teachers are dynamic bilingual educators who are adding to the linguistic repertoire that students bring into the classroom while working toward content mastery.

- Teachers across the continuum of bilingualism provide home language support as scaffolding when appropriate in adding to students' linguistic repertoires and facilitating content mastery.

Examples of Translanguaging	Not Examples of Translanguaging

FIGURE 7.1   *Translanguaging card sort activity, D. Witt*

DOI: 10.1057/9781137385765

Examples of translanguaging

A teacher introduces 2–3 key vocabulary words and their definitions at the beginning of the lesson and asks students to translate the definition into their home languages.	A teacher has students listen to a song in Spanish about the topic of the day. She then has them answer a series of questions about the song in English.
Teacher allows a student who is struggling to say something in English during a presentation to ask a classmate to translate what they are trying to say into English, which the student is then asked to repeat.	A teacher has students look at a series of pictures and asks students to discuss in small groups what they see and what they can infer. They can discuss in any language they wish but are asked to share with the whole class in English.

Examples of practices not considered translanguaging

The teacher speaks in English and then translates what she just said into Spanish after every few sentences.	A teacher does a word-for-word translation of a text and tells students to either read the English text or the text in their home language; all students choose to read the home language only or the English only text.
Students are given a reading that is chunked into paragraphs. The paragraphs alternate between one in English and an exact translation in their home language.	

FIGURE 7.1   *Continued*

that make teachers aware of the potential of translanguaging. Figure 7.1 is an example of one such activity – a Translanguaging Card Sort Activity to be used for professional development of teachers in these schools.

Unless teacher education programs acknowledge the potential of translanguaging in state-government-sponsored schools, translanguaging will remain an illicit pedagogical strategy used widely by teachers and students. To harness the potential of translanguaging as pedagogical practice in

DOI: 10.1057/9781137385765

order to educate the mostly bilingual students in our schools today, more is needed than simply accepting it. The next section describes a project in New York State that focuses on helping educators, and especially school leaders, understand the complex practices of bilinguals and use them to educate.

A translanguaging project in New York State for educators

The potential of a translanguaging pedagogy to develop more sophisticated discourse, deeper comprehension of texts, production of more complex texts, authentic and meaningful evaluation of what students know, as well as to question linguistic inequalities and to include the voices of learners who have been minoritized, is increasingly being recognized by educators. However, it is not always officially sanctioned by educational authorities. But even this is beginning to change. One example of these innovative implementational spaces is the City University of New York-New York State Initiative on Emergent Bilinguals (CUNY-NYSIEB, www.cuny-nysieb.org).[1] CUNY-NYSIEB encourages the collaboration of CUNY scholars with school leaders and teachers in failing schools that have large numbers of emergent bilinguals in order to incorporate translanguaging pedagogies (for a fuller description, see García and Menken, forthcoming). Among the resources developed by the project, is a teacher guide to translanguaging (Celic and Seltzer, 2012) with an introduction by García (2012).

The CUNY-NYSIEB project breaks away from the rigidity of program structures for emergent bilinguals and focuses on carving out spaces within schools to build on the complex and fluid ways that emergent bilinguals actually use language. Three tenets make up the CUNY-NYSIEB vision:

1   the creative *emergence* of individual language practices,
2   the *dynamics of bilingualism*, and
3   the *dynamic processes of teaching and learning* emergent bilinguals (for a complete statement of the vision, visit www.cuny-nysieb.org).

The CUNY-NYSIEB vision holds that bilingualism is the desired norm for all American students, and that rather than a 'problem', it is an asset that all students in New York State should possess to meet today's demands. Bilingual development is not linear, static or able to reach an ultimate end-point of completion; rather, it is always emergent, continuous, never-ending and shaped by relationships with people, texts and situations.

DOI: 10.1057/9781137385765

The work of CUNY-NYSIEB contests traditional views of bilinguals and bilingualism normed on the language practices of monolinguals. Translanguaging as the discursive norm of all bilinguals, as well as a pedagogical theory of learning and teaching, is the centerpiece of the CUNY-NYSIEB vision, asserting that emergent bilinguals need to perform fluid and dynamic language practices that go beyond separate conceptualizations of 'first' and 'second' languages. Two non-negotiable principles for schools emerge from the vision:

1   Bilingualism has to be used as a resource in education: Regardless of program structure, ALL the language practices of bilingual students are not only recognized but leveraged as a crucial instructional tool and, to the greatest extent possible, nurtured and developed. The entire linguistic repertoire of bilingual children is used flexibly and strategically in instruction in order to engage the children cognitively, academically, emotionally and creatively.
2   Support of a multilingual ecology for the whole school: The entire range of language practices of children and families are evident in the school's textual landscape (for example, in signs throughout the school, in texts in the library and classrooms), as well as in the interactions of all members of the school community. This extends beyond the language practices of emergent bilinguals to include those of ALL students in the school.

In the first two years of implementation, many changes in the CUNY-NYSIEB schools have occurred (see García and Sánchez, forthcoming). The examples of the schools' appropriations of multilingualism are many. Schools are transgressing the boundaries between the constructed monolingualism of the school and the multilingualism of the community, and are creating a translanguaging space. The multilingual ecology of the schools has totally been transformed. Figure 7.2 shows a multilingual bulletin board in one of the schools welcoming parents, but also translating common questions into Bengali, Arabic, Spanish, Urdu, Russian and Albanian, the languages of the school. This not only makes the parents feel welcomed, but also permits teachers to interact with parents in many languages, even if just pointing to the right question.

Figure 7.3 shows the efforts to which one school has gone to send announcements home to parents in the children's languages – English, Spanish, Vietnamese, Karen, French, Arabic and Bengali.

DOI: 10.1057/9781137385765

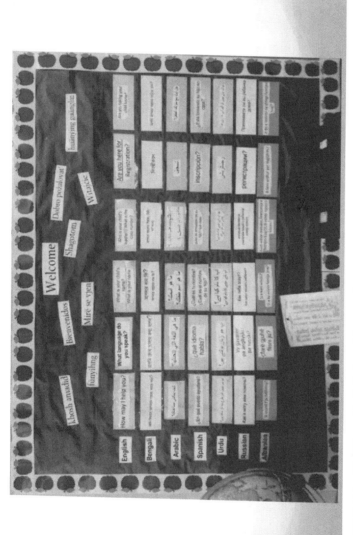

FIGURE 7.2 *Multilingual bulletin board for parents*

DOI: 10.1057/9781137385765

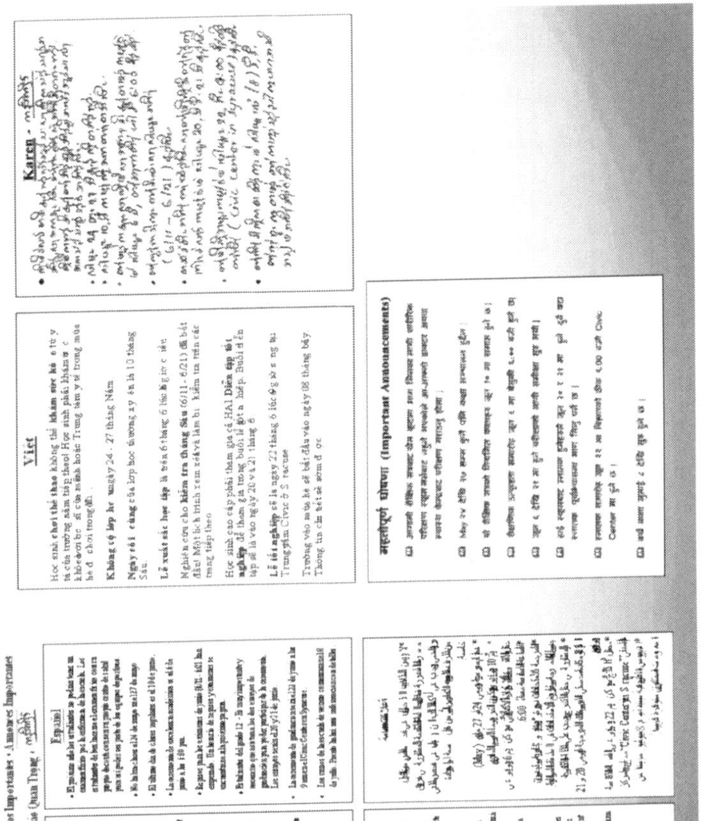

Important Announcements · Announces Importantes · Thông Báo Quan Trọng · ᨕᨘᨑᨗᨈᨗ

English

- Students must get attendance permission to participate in physical exams from the school nurse and the principal. Students MUST get physicals from the school nurse before they can participate in sports.
- On Cinco de Mayo, May 5th
- Last Day of Regular Classes is June 15
- The Awards & Distribution Ceremony is at 10am at 1pm.
- It is with the latest DANCE Graduation Rehearsals are scheduled to meet each at noon at the next page.

- Students must attend DANCE Graduation Rehearsals and to participate in the Graduation Ceremony. Rehearsals will be set June 20 and June 21.
- Graduation Ceremony will be June 22 at West of the Court will be at 6pm.
- It is now that school will be graduated right. More information will be available soon.

Français

"Les étudiants ne peuvent participer à un examen physique médicale, un autorisation de l'école. Il ne peut pas participer à ce sujet physique et tableaux des événements les participer à programme médicaux sociaux au-delà de l'école particulière.

"Il y a lieu le 5 mai

"Le dernier jour des Classes Régulières est le 15 juin

"La remise prix parcipate à la Cérémonie de la remise des diplômes. Les achèves du baccalauréat du lieu ne se feront aux entrées à 10h à page concerne.

"Pour ne peut pas participer à la Cérémonie de la remise des diplômes. Les parties de séances et ensuite les représentations. Ces répétitions seront définies le 20 et 21 juin.

"La Cérémonie de remise des diplômes le le 22 juin au West-Centre Group à 18 pm en 6 pm. Ces à partir de 18 heures à 18 pm.

"Le à l'école d'un moment particulier. D'un information sera disponible très bientôt.

Viet

Học sinh cần thiết thực hành không thể tham gia thi khám sức khỏe thể y tế của trường năm tiệp theo. Học sinh phải khám y tế trường màu sức khỏe trước khi có thể tham dự hoặc thể thao.

Khang cô lớp học ngày 24 – 27 tháng Năm

Ngày rồi rằng của lớp học thường xuyên là 15 tháng Sáu.

Lễ xuất sắc hạo tập là trên 6 tháng 6 lúc 10 giờ & 1 giờ.

Ngày kế cơn cho kiếm tra tháng Sáu (6/11, 6/21) đã bắt đầu một học trình ràm sẽ các nam kế lâm bổ. Thêm tin trên các trang tiếp theo.

Học sinh cần các phải tham gia lễ HAI Diễn tập một ngày lập để tham gia tại tông toại là giữa liệp. Buổi diễn tập sẽ vào ngày 20 và 21 tháng 6.

Lễ lái ra gồm số là ngày 22 tháng 6 tác bộ sổ số là ng tại Trung tâm Civic 6 5 racine.

Trường này mà lại sẽ tối đầu vào ngày 08 tháng bảy. Thông tin rằm tết sẽ sớm đã có.

Karen · ᨕᨘᨑᨗᨈᨗ

(handwritten Karen text, largely illegible)

Arabic

(Arabic text, largely illegible)

महत्वपूर्ण घोषणा (Important Announcements)

☐ (Hindi/Nepali text, largely illegible)

☐ ...

☐ ...

☐ ...

☐ ...

☐ ...

FIGURE 7.3   *Multilingual announcements for parents*

DOI: 10.1057/9781137385765

Beyond changes in the multilingual ecology, pedagogical practices are being transformed through a focus on translanguaging. Bilingual teachers who before never put one language alongside another, now bring them together, as in Figure 7.4, and use the charts to develop metalinguistic awareness and conduct language inquiries.

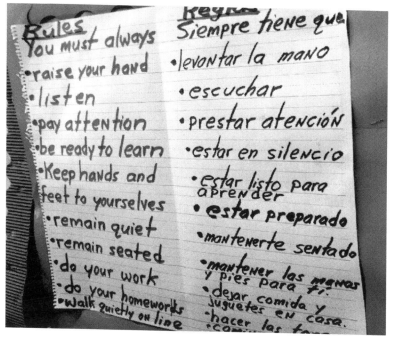

FIGURE 7.4   *Teacher's chart in English and Spanish*

This particular Chart of Class Rules was produced by the teacher and the children first in English. It is interesting to note that the rules in Spanish follow a different order and emphasize different things: being ready to learn in English, but '*estar en silencio*' [being quiet] in Spanish.

In both bilingual and English programs for emergent bilinguals, students are taught to annotate texts, as in Figure 7.5. Teachers also have multilingual texts readily available, and encourage students to find texts at home or on the Internet and bring them to class.

DOI: 10.1057/9781137385765

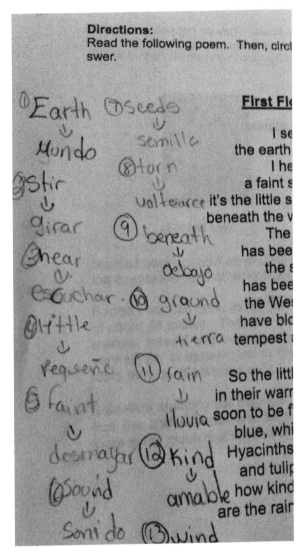

FIGURE 7.5   *Student's annotated text*

Table 7.2 displays recommendations for teachers to encourage their students' translanguaging, as well as their own. These recommendations are adaptations of those developed by Sarah Hesson, a member of the CUNY-NYSIEB team.

DOI: 10.1057/9781137385765

TABLE 7.2 *Recommendations for translanguaging (developed by S. Hesson with adaptation by O. García)*

When students are ...

Reading
- ▶ Assign bilingual reading partners for mutual assistance.
- ▶ Provide multilingual books/translations of books whenever possible.
- ▶ Provide/encourage multilingual reading material for research projects.

Writing
- ▶ Allow students to audio record ideas first using all their language resources, before writing.
- ▶ Assign students bilingual writing partners for mutual assistance.
- ▶ Have students pre-write using all their language resources, then select one language/voice in which to publish it.
- ▶ Have students experiment with translanguaging in writing for bilingual audiences, and then for monolingual audiences.

Speaking
- ▶ Assign language partners in class (beginner with intermediate, etc.).
- ▶ Assign newcomers a buddy to show them around, answer questions, etc.
- ▶ Group students so they can use the same language resources in small group work.
- ▶ Group students so that they have to use other language resources to make themselves understood.

Listening
- ▶ Create a multilingual listening center comprised of fiction and non-fiction texts in the classroom, narratives of community members, and books recorded by students or their families (a favorite book or their own writing).
- ▶ Allow students to explain things to each other using all their language resources.

When teacher is ...

Reading
- ▶ During content area reading, give partners time to discuss difficult passages or words in home language or using all their resources.
- ▶ Create a multilingual interactive word wall (especially in content areas – Math, Science, Social Studies).

Writing
- ▶ Write instructions in as many languages as possible, using translanguaging in the written text.
- ▶ Write on the board in one language or the other, as student(s) give ideas in any language.
- ▶ Give comments on an assignment in home language or modeling translanguaging in writing.
- ▶ Make connections between words to build vocabulary and improve spelling, especially through cognates (for example, revolución → revolution; triángulo → triangle).

Speaking
- ▶ Use Preview (other language)-View (language of lesson)-Review (other language) to facilitate understanding/language learning.
- ▶ Conduct individual conferences with students using translanguaging to ensure understanding, to make language connections (in grammar, vocabulary, etc.), and to model translanguaging.

Listening
- ▶ Allow students to explain/share ideas using all their languages (another student can translate if you or the class doesn't speak the language).
- ▶ Use the language structures checklist (Celic, 2009) to track what you hear in both languages.

DOI: 10.1057/9781137385765

Despite recent efforts to educate teachers and school leaders about the advantages of using translanguaging in classrooms, challenges remain. Two of the most important challenges have to do with the ways in which translanguaging is taken up by most educators. Although increasingly accepted as scaffolding practice in the teaching of the standard academic language, translanguaging is rarely accepted as a legitimate practice that students should understand how to do. Although used in teaching, it is rarely used in assessment. The next section considers these two main challenges.

Challenges for translanguaging and education: teaching to do and assessments

The challenge of teaching to do translanguaging

Although translanguaging as pedagogy is being increasingly used by teachers, whether in sanctioned or unsanctioned situations, it is rare to actually find schooling situations in which students' understanding of how to do translanguaging as a legitimate practice is being developed. As Canagarajah (2011a) writes:

> A further set of questions relate to the possibility of teaching translanguaging in classrooms. The pedagogical side is underdeveloped in general. While we have studied the practice of translanguaging in social life – i.e., in urban youth encounters, linguistic landscapes, and the Internet – we haven't figured out how to develop such proficiency among students in classrooms. (8)

If translanguaging is an important ability for all students, then the question becomes: Where does one learn to do translanguaging? How does one learn to practice translanguaging? Is it enough to provide translanguaging spaces in schools and communities where children develop this expertise on their own? Or do schools need to do more that just acknowledge and leverage translanguaging practices to develop 'standard' language practices for academic contexts? Can those academic contexts also accommodate translanguaging for its own sake?

Translanguaging contests and transcends all scripts of the larger dominant society. It incorporates difference, pluralities and the languaging of everyday to produce and legitimize learning. Students would be

DOI: 10.1057/9781137385765

encouraged to design their own texts, using their own languaging practices, for self-awareness and self-healing as individuals and members of minoritized communities. These translanguaged texts could then serve as counter-texts and be used to interrogate language practices in schools that sustain relations of power and privilege.

Given the potential of translanguaging as alternate critical texts, it is then unlikely that schools will accommodate translanguaging as more than what it is today, an *adaptive* space. An *established* translanguaging space in schools would require more. It would demand that we stop penalizing students who translanguage, extending this ability to all. And it would authorize the translanguaging norm of bilingual communities as a meaning-making mechanism and language practice, of equal value to the 'standard' norm in academic contexts. It would require that translanguaging practices be accepted, for example, in assessment, since a bilingual student's linguistic repertoire cannot be measured in a single constructed standard language (see García, 2009a, chapter 15; Shohamy, 2001, 2011). It would entail, in other words, that we structure learning, teaching and assessment, taking into account the tension of different meaning-making signs so as to expand and integrate the social spaces that, despite much translanguaging, remain separate today in a hierarchy of power.

The challenge of using translanguaging in assessment

In most of the world today, policy makers view assessment as the main catalyst to improve the education of students. Assessments should help teachers make meaningful instructional decisions. However, standardized assessments are usually administered in one language only, confounding knowledge with language ability. This is especially troubling for bilingual students, and especially for those at the beginning points of the bilingual continuum (Kieffer, Lesaux and Snow, 2008). In the few cases when multilingual summative assessments are available (for example, New York State translates some year-end exams into five languages), students are required to make a choice of language. In these cases, students may be given two exam papers – one in the dominant language and the other in the home language of the student – but responses are valid only in one language. This is again a reflection of a monoglossic view of bilingualism as parallel monolingualisms (Heller, 2007).

DOI: 10.1057/9781137385765

And yet, if translanguaging were an accepted language practice, standardized assessments would be done in translanguaged ways, using the advanced adaptive technologies that have been developed (see García, 2009a, chapter 15 for more on this). In these translanguaged-mode assessments, questions would be posed in many languages from which students would choose, and students would be free to reply with whatever multilingual multimodal practices that would display their understandings and knowledge. Assessments using a translanguaging mode would enable students to show what they know using their entire linguistic repertoire. If, on the other hand, teachers wanted to assess different language practices, including the use of standard oral and written language, the assessment would then randomly change the language and mode of the question, as well as request different language practices for replies, including various modes or language practices. Despite the potential of translanguaged assessments, and the ability of today's advanced technology to develop these adaptive tests, they do not exist. Although translanguaging in assessment has the potential to truly assess what students know how to do both conceptually and linguistically without limits imposed by external societal definitions of standard language, these tests have not been developed. This casts doubt as to the intentions of policy makers, since the consequence of monolingual standardized tests becomes the highlighting of differences among those who language differently and the rendering of those differences as deficiencies. By only considering the practices of the monolingual elite as the norm, bilingual languaging is rendered illegitimate and deficient. Assessment scores are then used to justify inequalities among class, racial, ethnic and linguistic groups.

It is more probable that translanguaging be used in performance-based assessment of the formative kind used by teachers, especially in what is known as dynamic assessment. Rather than solely documenting student performance, dynamic assessment, based on the interactive nature of development posited by Vygotsky (1978), embeds instruction within assessment and determines the range at which the student performs. It would then be possible for teachers to engage students in translanguaging events as they assess students' languaging and knowledge-making, regardless of language form. But even teachers who are committed to formative dynamic assessments are often unwilling to use translanguaging in assessment.

Translanguaging goes against the grain of the kind of language use that many expect from students and teachers. Translanguaging in assessment

DOI: 10.1057/9781137385765

is then not accepted either by the policy makers who commission the development of tests nor by many teachers who have been taught to assess knowledge in accordance with artificial bounds of social norms and language. Accepting translanguaging in assessment would require a change in epistemology that is beyond the limits of what most schools (and teachers) permit and value today.

As we have seen, beyond the promise of translanguaging there are challenges. We know how to use translanguaging to learn, teach and assess. But dominant language ideologies often prevent even well-meaning bilingual teachers from embracing translanguaging to teach and assess.

Note

1   CUNY-NYSIEB is funded by the New York State Education Department and is a project initiated by Arlen Benjamin-Gómez. The Principal Investigator is Prof. Ricardo Otheguy, with co-Principal Investigators Ofelia García, Kate Menken and Tatyana Kleyn (6/2013-6/2014). At its inception Nelson Flores served as Acting Project Coordinator, a position now held by Dr. María Teresa Sánchez. The team of the Leadership component in 2012–2014 is composed of the following CUNY faculty: Professors Laura Ascenzi-Moreno, Brian Collins, Ann Ebe, Cecilia Espinosa, Tatyana Kleyn and Vanessa Pérez; a Field Supervisor, Christina Celic; and Research Assistants: Kathryn Carpenter, Ivana Espinet, Luis Guzmán, Luz Herrera, Sarah Hesson, Liza Pappas, María Peña, Kate Seltzer and Heather Woodley.

DOI: 10.1057/9781137385765

Conclusion

Abstract: *The short conclusion reminds readers that translanguaging extends our traditional definitions of language and bilingualism and disrupts traditional boundaries; and although important in mediating complex social and cognitive activities, it is seldom used in schools. The conclusion reminds readers of the potential of translanguaging as a way to produce trans-spaces and trans-subjects capable of transforming subjectivities, social and cognitive structures and the sociopolitical order, as well as to liberate language and bilingualism from the societal constraints in which it has been held by monolingual and monoglossic ideologies.*

Keywords: bilingual education; bilingualism; translanguaging

García, Ofelia, and Li Wei. *Translanguaging: Language, Bilingualism and Education.* Basingstoke: Palgrave Macmillan, 2014. DOI: 10.1057/9781137385765.

DOI: 10.1057/9781137385765

This book has considered the meanings of translanguaging and what a translanguaging approach means for language, on the one hand, and for education on the other. Translanguaging extends our traditional definitions of language and bilingualism. It refers to the ways in which bilinguals use their complex semiotic repertoire to act, to know, and to be. Through multiple discursive practices that constitute the language users' linguistic repertories, translanguaging makes visible the different histories, identities, heritages and ideologies of the multilingual language users. In integrating the act of languaging, doing and knowing, translanguaging reflects the goal of education itself. Yet although translanguaging is an apt tool to mediate complex social and cognitive activities, it is seldom used in schools in any systematic way. We need to question why this is so, as we continue to use translanguaging in schools to ensure that students, and especially bilingual students, learn to construct an equitable and generous meaning-making space.

The practice of translanguaging is not only based on a trans-semiotic system, it also produces trans-spaces. In producing a trans-subject, translanguaging is capable of trans-forming subjectivities and identities, cognitive and social structures and the sociopolitical order. The transdisciplinarity associated with translanguaging enables us to broaden our disciplinary lens, bringing a simultaneous sociocultural–sociocognitive approach to the study of doing language and learning. The continuous becoming of translanguaging opens up a space of limitless possibilities for speakers and learners, which promises a more just world.

Although our focus in this book has been on language and education, the implications of adopting a translanguaging lens go way beyond these spheres. Translanguaging permeates our everyday lives. In the superdiverse world of the 21st century, people increasingly live their lives in more than one place, often beyond national borders. And they are exposed to and follow diverse national and cultural traditions. The individuals involved in the process, or the transnationals, often develop meaningful ties to more than one home country, blurring the congruence of social space and geographical space. They challenge many long-held assumptions about membership, development and equity. To understand the lives of the transnationals requires an analytic shift that entails letting go of methodological nationalism or the expectation that social life logically and automatically takes place within the nation-state framework, and instead, locating transnationals within the social fields in which they may or may

DOI: 10.1057/9781137385765

not be embedded. A translanguaging lens enables us to break traditional boundaries. It is not only apt to describe the languaging practices of bilinguals and multilinguals, but also has the capacity to liberate bilingualism, multilingualism and plurilingualism from the societal constraints in which it has been held by monolingual and monoglossic ideologies. Translanguaging enables us to imagine new ways of being and languaging so that we can begin to act differently upon the world.

DOI: 10.1057/9781137385765

References

Adams, J. N. (2003) *Bilingualism and the Latin Language* (Cambridge: Cambridge University Press).

Adelman Reyes, S. and Kleyn, T. (2010) *Teaching in Two Languages. A Guide for K-12 Bilingual Educators.* (Thousand Oaks, CA: Corwin Press).

Althusser, L. (1972) 'Ideology and Ideological State Apparatuses' in *Lenin and Philosophy and Other Essays* (Monthly Review Press).

Angelova, M., Gunawardena, D. and Volk, D. (2006) 'Peer Teaching and Learning: Co-Constructing Language in a Dual Language First Grade', *Language and Education*, 20(3), 173–190.

Annamalai, E. (2005) 'Nation-Building in a Globalized World: Language Choice and Education in India' in A. M. Y. Lin and P. W. Martin (eds) *Decolonisation, Globalisation. Language-in-Education Policy and Practice* (Clevedon, UK: Multilingual Matters).

Anton, M. and DiCamilla, F. (1998) 'Socio-Cognitive Functions of L1 Collaborative Interaction in the L2 Classroom', *The Canadian Modern Language Review*, 54(3), 314–342.

Anzaldúa, G. (1987) *Borderlands/La Frontera. The New Mestiza* (San Francisco: Aunt Lute Books).

Arnheim, R. (1969) *Visual Thinking* (Berkeley, CA: University of California Press).

Arthur, J. and Martin, P. (2006) 'Accomplishing Lessons in Postcolonial Classrooms: Comparative Perspectives from Botswana and Brunei Darussalam', *Comparative Education*, 42, 177–202.

DOI: 10.1057/9781137385765

Auer, P. (1999) *Code-Switching in Conversation: Language Interactions and Identity* (London: Routledge).

Auer, P. (2005) 'A Postscript: Code-Switching and Social Identity', *Journal of Pragmatics*, 37(3), 403–410.

Baetens, Beardsmore H. (2009) 'Bilingual Education: Factors and Variables' in O. García (ed.) *Bilingual Education in the 21st Century: A Global Perspective* (Malden, MA: Wiley/Blackwell).

Bailey, B. (2007) 'Heteroglossia and Boundaries' in M. Heller (ed.) *Bilingualism: A Social Approach* (Basingstoke, UK: Palgrave), pp. 257–276.

Baker, C. (2001) *Foundations of Bilingual Education and Bilingualism*, 3rd edn (Clevedon, UK: Multilingual Matters).

Baker, C. (2011) *Foundations of Bilingual Education and Bilingualism*, 5th edn (Bristol, UK: Multilingual Matters).

Bakhtin, M. (1981) *Dialogic Imagination: Four Essays* (Austin, TX: University of Texas Press).

Bartlett, L. and García, O. (2011) *Additive Schooling in Subtractive Times. Bilingual Education and Dominican Immigrant Youth in the Heights* (Tennessee: Vanderbilt University Press).

Becker, A. L. (1988) 'Language in Particular: A Lecture', in D. Tannen (ed.) *Linguistics in Context* (Norwood, NJ: Ablex), pp. 17–35.

Becker, A. L. (1995) *Beyond Translation: Essays toward a Modern Philosophy* (Ann Arbor: University of Michigan Press).

Bezemer, J. and Kress, G. (2008) 'Writing in Multimodal Texts: A Social Semiotic Account of Designs Teacher Instructions', *Linguistics and Education*, 19, 166–178.

Bhabha, H. K. (1994) *The Location of Culture* (New York and London: Routledge).

Bialystok, E., Craik, F. I. M., Klein, R. and Viswanathan, M. (2004) 'Bilingualism, Aging, and Cognitive Control: Evidence From the Simon Task', *Psychology and Aging*, 19(2), 290–303.

Blackledge, A. and Creese, A. (2010) *Multilingualism: A Critical Perspective* (London: Continuum).

Blommaert, J. (2010) *The Sociolinguistics of Globalization* (Cambridge: Cambridge University Press).

Bonfiglio, T. H. (2010) *Mother Tongues and Nations. The Invention of the Native Speaker* (New York: Mouton de Gruyter).

Borges, J. L. (1971) *The Aleph and Other Stories: 1993–1969* (New York: Bantam Books).

DOI: 10.1057/9781137385765

Bosch, L. and Sebastian-Galles, N. (1997) 'Native-Language Recognition Abilities in 4-Month-Old Infants from Monolingual and Bilingual Environments', *Cognition*, 65, 33–69.

Bourdieu, P. (1991) *Language and Symbolic Power* (Cambridge, MA: Harvard University Press).

Bourdieu, P. and Passeron, J. C. (1990) *Reproduction in Education, Society and Culture* (London: Sage).

Brantmeier, E. J. (n.d.) *Empowerment Pedagogy: Co-learning and Teaching*, http://www.indiana.edu/~leeehman/Brantmeier.pdf

Brinton, D., Kagan, O. and Bauhaus, S. (eds) (2007) *Heritage Language Education: A New Field Emerging* (London: Routledge).

Brock-Utne, B. (2006) 'English as the Language of Instruction or Destruction – How Do Teachers and Students in Tanzania Cope?' in A. Weidemann and B. Smieja (eds) *Empowerment through Language and Education: Cases and Case Studies from North America, Europe, Africa and Japan* (Frankfurt: Peter Lang), pp. 75–91.

Brubacker, R. (2009) 'Ethnicity, Race and Nationalism', *Annual Review of Sociology*, 35, 21–42.

Brutt-Griffler, J. (2002) *World English: A Study of its Development* (Clevedon, UK: Multilingual Matters).

Bunyi, G. (2005) 'Language Practices in Kenya' in A. M. Lin and P. W. Martin (eds) *Decolonisation, Globalisation. Language-in-Education Policy and Practice* (Clevedon, UK: Multilingual Matters), pp. 31–152.

Burton-Roberts, N. (2004) 'Linguistic Diversity in a Universalist Context: Language Thought and Culture' in R. Talif, S. H. Chan, B. E. Wong, A. N. Abdullah and R. Noor (eds) *Beyond Barriers, Fresh Frontiers: Selected Readings on Languages, Literatures, and Cultures* (Serdang Selangor: Universiti Putra Malaysia Press), pp. 112–124.

Busch, B. (2011) 'Building on Heteroglossia and Heterogeneity: The Experience of a Multilingual Classroom', presentation held at the 3rd International Conference on Language, Education and Diversity (LED), 22–25 November 2011, *Colloquium: Language, Education, and Superdiversity*, University of Auckland, New Zealand.

Canagarajah, S. (ed.) (2005) *Reclaiming the Local in Language Policy and Practice* (Mahwah, NJ: Lawrence Erlbaum).

Canagarajah, S. (2007) 'The Ecology of Global English', *International Multilingual Research Journal*, 1(2), 89–100.

DOI: 10.1057/9781137385765

Canagarajah, S. (2011a) 'Codemeshing in Academic Writing: Identifying Teachable Strategies of Translanguaging', *The Modern Language Journal*, 95, 401–417.

Canagarajah, S. (2011b) 'Translanguaging in the Classroom: Emerging Issues for Research and Pedagogy' in Li Wei (ed.) *Applied Linguistics Review, Volume 2* (Berlin, Germany: De Gruyter Mouton), pp. 1–27.

Canagarajah, S. (2013) *Translingual Practice: Global Englishes and Cosmopolitan Relations* (London: Routledge).

Celic, C. (2009) *English Language Learners Day by Day K-6. A Complete Guide to Literacy, Content-Area, and Language Instruction* (Portsmouth, New Hampshire: Heinemann).

Celic, C. and Seltzer, K. (2012) *Translanguaging: A CUNY-NYSIEB Guide for Educators*, http://www.cuny-nysieb.org

Cenoz, J. (2009) *Towards Multilingual Education. Basque Educational Research from an International Perspective* (Bristol, UK: Multilingual Matters).

Ch'ien, E. M. N. (2005) *Weird English* (Cambridge, MA: Harvard University Press).

Chomsky, Noam (1966). *Cartesian Linguistics: A Chapter in the History of Rationalist Thought.* New York: Harper & Row.

Chomsky, N. (1988) *Language and Problems of Knowledge* (Cambridge: MIT Press).

Chomsky, N. (1995) 'Bare Phrase' in H. Campos and P. Kempshinsky (eds) *Evolution and Revolution in Linguistic Theory: Essays in Honor of Carlos P. Otero* (Washington: Georgetown University Press), pp. 51–109.

Clyne, M. (2003) *Dynamics of Language Contact* (Cambridge: Cambridge University Press).

Cook, V. J. (2008) *Second Language Learning and Language Teaching* (London: Arnold).

Cook, V. J. (2012) 'Multi-Competence' in C. Chapelle (ed.) *The Encyclopedia of Applied Linguistics* (Oxford: Wiley-Blackwell).

Cook, V. J. and Bassetti, B. (eds) (2011) *Language and Bilingual Cognition* (New York: Psychology Press).

Cook, V. J. and Li Wei (eds) (forthcoming) *The Cambridge Handbook of Linguistic Competence* (Cambridge: Cambridge University Press).

Costa, A. and Santesteban, M. (2004) 'Lexical Access in Bilingual Speech Production: Evidence from Language Switching in Highly Proficient Bilinguals and L2 Learners', *Journal of Memory and Language*, 50, 491–511.

DOI: 10.1057/9781137385765

Council of Europe (2000) *Common European Framework of Reference for Languages: Learning, Teaching, Assessment*, http://www.coe.int/t/dg4/linguistic/CADRE_EN.asp

Coyle D., Hood, P. and Marsh, D. (2010) *CLIL. Content and Language Integrated Learning* (Cambridge: Cambridge University Press).

Creese, A. and Blackledge, A. (2010) 'Translanguaging in the Bilingual Classroom: A Pedagogy for Learning and Teaching? *Modern Language Journal*, 94(i), 103–115.

Creese, A. and Martin, P. (eds) (2003) *Multilingual Classroom Ecologies* (Clevedon, UK: Multilingual Matters).

Cummins, J. (1979) 'Cognitive/Academic Language Proficiency, Linguistic Interdependence, the Optimum Age Question, and Some Other Matters', *Working Papers on Bilingualism*, 19, 121–129.

Cummins, J. (1981) 'The Role of Primary Language Development in Promoting Educational Success for Language Minority Students' in California State Department of Education (ed.) *Schooling and Language Minority Students: A Theoretical Framework* (Los Angeles, CA: Evaluation, Dissemination and Assessment Center), pp. 3–50.

Cummins, J. (2005) 'A Proposal for Action: Straregies for Recognizing Heritage Language Competence as a Learning Resource within the Mainstream Classroom', *Modern Language Journal*, 89(5), 585–592.

Cummins, J. (2007) 'Rethinking Monolingual Instructional Strategies in Multilingual Classrooms', *The Canadian Journal of Applied Linguistics*, 10(2), 221–240.

Cummins, J. (2008) 'Teaching for Transfer: Challenging the Two Solitudes Assumption in Bilingual Education' in J. Cummins and N. H. Hornberger (eds) *Encyclopedia of Language and Education, 2nd Edition, Volume 5: Bilingual Education* (New York: Springer), pp. 65–75.

Cummins, J. and Danesi, M. (1990) *Heritage Languages. The Development and Denial of Canada's Linguistic Resources* (Montreal: Our Schools/Our Selves Education Foundation).

Cummins, J. and Early, M. (2011) *Identity Texts: The Collaborative Creation of Power in Multilingual Schools* (Stoke-on-Trent, UK: Trentham Books).

Danesi, M., McLeod, K. A. and Morris, S. (1993) *Heritage Languages and Education: The Canadian Experience* (Oakville/New York/London: Mosaic Press).

Davies B. and Harré, R. (1990) 'Positioning: The Discursive Production of Selves', *Journal for the Theory of Social Behaviour*, 20(1), 43–63.

DOI: 10.1057/9781137385765

De Bot, K., Lowie, W. and Verspoor, M. (2007) 'A Dynamic Systems Theory Approach to Second Language Acquisition', *Bilingualism Language and Cognition*, 10(1), 7–21.

De Groot, A. M. B. (2011) *Language and Cognition in Bilinguals and Multilinguals: An Introduction* (New York and Hove: Psychology Press).

Del Valle, J. (2000) 'Monoglossic Policies for a Heteroglossic Culture: Misinterpreted Multilingualism in Modern Galicia', *Language and Communication*, 20, 105–132.

Delpit, L. (2006) *Other People's Children: Cultural Conflict in the Classroom* (New York: The New Press).

Díaz, J. (2007) *The Brief Wondrous Life of Oscar Wao* (New York: Riverhead Books).

Díaz, J. (2013) 'We Exist in a Constant State of Translation. We Just Don't Like It'. *The Bar Buenos Aires Review*, Interview by Karen Cresci, 4 May 2013, http://www.buenosairesreview.org/2013/05/diaz-constant-state-of-translation/#

DiCamilla, F. J. and Antón, M. (2004) 'Private Speech: A Study of Language for Thought in the Collaborative Interaction of Language Learners', *International Journal of Applied Linguistics*, 14, 36–69.

Dijkstra T. and Van Heuven W. J. B. (2002) 'The Architecture of the Bilingual Word Recognition System: From Identification to Decision', *Bilingualism: Language and Cognition*, 5, 175–197.

Dijkstra T., Van Jaarsveld H. and Ten Brinke, S. (1998) 'Interlingual Homograph Recognition: Effects of Task Demands and Language Intermixing', *Bilingualism: Language and Cognition*, 1, 51–66.

Edelsky, C. (1989) 'Bilingual Children's Writing: Fact and Fiction' in D. M. Johnson and D. H. Roen (eds) *Richness in Writing: Empowering ESL Students* (New York: Longman), pp. 165–176.

Elman, J. L., Bates, E. A., Johnson, M. H., Karmiloff-Smith, A., Parisi, D. and Plunkett, K. (1996) *Rethinking Innateness: A Connectionist Perspective on Development* (Cambridge, MA: The MIT Press).

Enfield, N. and Levinson, S. (eds) (2006) *Roots of Human Sociality: Culture, Cognition and Interaction* (Oxford: Berg).

Escamilla, K., Hopewell, S., Butvilofsky, S., Sparrow, W., Soltero-González, L., Ruiz-Figueroa, O. and Escamilla, M. (2013) *Biliteracy from the Start: Literacy Squared in Action* (Philadelphia, PA: Caslon).

Fabbro, F. (2001) 'The Bilingual Brain: Cerebral Representation of Languages', *Brain and Language*, 79(2), 211–222.

DOI: 10.1057/9781137385765

Fishman, J. A. (1966) *Language Loyalty in the United States. The Maintenance and Perpetuation of Non-English Mother Tongues by American Ethnic and Religious Groups* (The Hague: Mouton).

Fishman, J. A., Cooper, R. L. and Ma, R. (1971) *Bilingualism in the Barrio* (Bloomington, IN: Indiana University Press).

Fitts, S. (2006) 'Reconstructing the Status Quo: Linguistic Interaction in a Dual-Language School', *Bilingual Research Journal*, 29(2), 337–365.

Fitts, S. (2009) 'Exploring Third Space in a Dual Language Setting: Opportunities and Challenges', *Journal of Latinos and Education*, 8(2), 87–104.

Flores, N. (2012) *From Nation-States to Neoliberalism: Language Ideologies and Governmentality*, Doctoral Dissertation (The Graduate Center, The City University of New York).

Flores, N. (2013) 'The Unexamined Relationship Between Neoliberalism and Plurilingualism: A Cautionary Tale', *TESOL Quarterly*, 47(3), 500–520.

Flores, N. and García, O. (2013) 'Linguistic Third Spaces in Education: Teachers' Translanguaging Across the Bilingual Continuum' in D. Little, C. Leung and P. Van Avermaet (eds) *Managing Diversity in Education: Key Issues and Some Responses* (Clevedon, UK: Multilingual Matters), pp. 243–256.

Foucault, M. (1972) *Archeology of Knowledge*. New York: Pantheon.

Foucault, M. (1986) 'Of Other Spaces', *Diacritics*, 16, 22–27.

Franceschini, R. (2011) 'Multilingualism and Multicompetence: A Conceptual View', *Modern Language Journal*, 95, 344–355.

Freire, P. (1974) *Pedagogy of the Oppressed* (New York: Continuum).

Fu, D. (2003) *An Island of English. Teaching ESL in Chinatown* (Portsmouth, NH: Heinemann).

Fu, D. (2009) *Writing Between Languages: How English Language Learners Make the Transition to Fluency, Grades 4-12* (Portsmouth, NH: Heinemann).

Gajo, L. (2007) 'Linguistic Knowledge and Subject Knowledge: How Does Bilingualism Contribute to Subject Development?', *International Journal of Bilingual Education and Bilingualism*, 10(5), 563–581.

García, O. (2009a) *Bilingual Education in the 21st Century: A Global Perspective* (Malden, MA and Oxford: Wiley/Blackwell).

García, O. (2009b) 'Reimagining Bilinguals in Education for the 21st Century', NALDIC (National Association for Language

DOI: 10.1057/9781137385765

Development in the Curriculum), *17th Annual Conference: Integrated language, Integrated Curriculum*, http://www.youtube.com/watch?v=rVI41CMw6HM

García, O. (2011a) 'Educating New York's bilingual children: Constructing a future from the past' *International Journal of Bilingual Education and Bilingualism* 14:2, 133–153.

García, O. (2011b) 'From Language Garden to Sustainable Languaging: Bilingual Education in a Global World', *Perspectives. A Publication of the National Association for Bilingual Education,* Sept./Oct. 2011, 5–10.

García, O. (with Makar, C., Starcevic, M. and Terry, A.) (2011c) 'Translanguaging of Latino Kindergarteners' in K. Potowski and J. Rothman (eds) *Bilingual Youth: Spanish in English Speaking Societies* (Amsterdam: John Benjamins), pp. 33–55.

García, O. (2012) 'Theorizing Translanguaging for Educators' in Celic, C. and Seltzer, K. *Translanguaging: A CUNY-NYSIEB Guide for Educators*, http://www.nysieb.ws.gc.cuny.edu/files/2013/03/Translanguaging-Guide-March-2013.pdf

García, O. (2013) 'From Diglossia to Transglossia: Bilingual and Multilingual Classrooms in the 21st Century' in C. Abello-Contesse, P. Chandler, M. D. López-Jiménez, M. M. Torreblanc López and R. Chacón Beltrán (eds) *Bilingualism and Multilingualism in School Settings* (Bristol: Multilingual Matters), pp. 155–178.

García, O. (2014a) 'Countering the Dual: Transglossia, Dynamic Bilingualism and Translanguaging in Education' in R. Rubdy and L. Alsagoff (eds) *The Global-Local Interface, Language Choice and Hybridity* (Bristol: Multilingual Matters), pp. 100–118.

García, O. (with Leiva, C.) (2014b) 'Theorizing and Enacting Translanguaging for Social Justice' in Creese, A. and Blackledge, A. *Heteroglossia as Practice and Pedagogy* (New York: Springer).

García, O., Bartlett, L. and Kleifgen, J. A. (2007) 'From Biliteracy to Pluriliteracies' in P. Auer and Li Wei (eds) *Handbook of Applied Linguistics,* Vol. 5: *Multilingualism* (Berlin: Mouton/de Gruyter), pp. 207–228.

García, O. and Flores, N. (2014) 'Multilingualism and Common Core State Standards in the US' in May, S. *The Multilingual Turn: Implications for SLA, TESOL, and Bilingual Education* (New York: Routledge), pp. 147–166.

García, O., Flores, N. and Woodley, H. H. (2012) 'Transgressing Monolingualism and Bilingual Dualities: Translanguaging

DOI: 10.1057/9781137385765

Pedagogies' in A. Yiakoumetti (ed.) *Harnessing Linguistic Variation for Better Education* (Bern: Peter Lang), pp. 45–76.

García, O., Flores N. and Woodley, H. H. (forthcoming) 'Constructing In-Between Spaces to "Do" Bilingualism: A Tale of Two High Schools in One City' in J. Cenoz and D. Gorter (eds) *Multilingualism in Education: New Directions.* (Cambridge: Cambridge University Press).

García, O., Ibarra-Johnson, S. and Seltzer, K. (forthcoming) *The Translanguaging Classroom* (Philadelphia: Caslon).

García, O. and Kano, N. (forthcoming) 'Translanguaging as Process and Pedagogy: Developing the English Writing of Japanese Students in the US' in J. Conteh and G. Meier (eds) *The Multilingual Turn in Languages Education: Benefits for Individuals and Societies* (Clevedon, UK: Multilingual Matters).

García, O. and Kleifgen, J. (2010) *Educating Emergent Bilinguals. Policies, Programs and Practices for English Language Learners* (New York: Teachers College Press).

García, O. and Kleyn, T. (2013) 'Teacher Education for Multilingual Education' in C. A. Chapelle (ed.) *Encyclopedia of Applied Linguistics* (Oxford, UK: Wiley-Blackwell), pp. 5543–5548.

García, O. and Menken, K. (forthcoming) 'Culivating an Ecology of Multilingualism in Schools' in B. Spolsky, O. Inbar and M. Tannenbaum (eds) *Challenges for Language Education and Policy: Making Space for People* (New York: Routledge).

García, O. and Otheguy, R. (forthcoming) 'Hispanic Bilingualism' in M. Lacorte (ed.) *The Routledge Handbook of Hispanic Applied Linguistics* (New York: Routledge).

García, O. and Sánchez, M. (forthcoming) 'Transforming Schools with Emergent Bilinguals: The CUNY-NYSIEB Project' in I. Dirim, I. Gogolin, D. Knorr, M. Krüger-Potratz, D. Lengyel, H. Reich and W. Weiße (eds) *Intercultural Education. Festschrift for Ulla Neumann* (Berlin: Waxmann-Verlag).

García, O. and Sylvan, C. (2011) 'Pedagogies and practices in multilingual classrooms: Singularities in Pluralities', *Modern Language Journal*, 95(iii), 385–400.

García, O., Zakharia, Z. and Otcu, B. (eds) (2013) *Bilingual Community Education for American Children: Beyond Heritage Languages in a Global City* (Bristol, UK: Multilingual Matters).

Goffman, E. (1979) *Gender Advertisements* (New York: Macmillan).

DOI: 10.1057/9781137385765

Goral, M., Levy, E., Obler, L. and Cohen, E. (2006) 'Cross-Language Lexical Connections in the Mental Lexicon: Evidence from a Case of Trilingual Aphasia', *Brain and Language*, 98, 235–247.

Gort, M. (2006) 'Strategic Codeswitching, Interliteracy, and Other Phenomena of Emergent Bilingual Writing: Lessons from First Grade Dual Language Classrooms', *Journal of Early Childhood Literacy*, 6(3), 323–354.

Gorter, D. (ed.) (2006) *Linguistic Landscape: A New Approach to Multilingualism* (Clevedon, UK: Multilingual Matters).

Green, D. (1986) 'Control, Activation, and Resource: A Framework and a Model for the Control of Speech in Bilinguals', *Brain and Language*, 27, 210–223.

Grosjean, F. (1982) *Life with Two Languages* (Cambridge, MA: Harvard University Press).

Grosjean, F. (2004) 'Stuying Bilinguals: Methodological and Conceptual Issues' in Bhatia, T.K. and Ritchie, W. C. (eds) *The Handbook of Bilingualism* (Malden, MA: Blackwell), pp. 32–63.

Grosjean, F. (2012) *Bilingual Life and Reality* (Cambridge, MA: Harvard University Press).

Gumperz, J. and Cook-Gumperz, J. (2005) 'Making Space for Bilingual Communicative Practice', *Intercultural Pragmatics*, 2(1), 1–23.

Gutiérrez, K. (2008) 'Developing a Sociocritical Literacy in the Third Space', *Reading Research Quarterly*, 43, 148–164.

Gutiérrez, K., Baquedano-López, P. and Alvarez, H. (2001) 'Literacy as Hybridity: Moving Beyond Bilingualism in Urban Classrooms' in M. de la Luz Reyes and J. J. Halcón (eds) *The Best for Our Children. Critical Perspectives on Literacy for Latino Students* (New York: Teachers College Press), pp. 122–141.

Gutiérrez, K. D., Baquedano-López, P. and Tejeda, C. (1999) 'Rethinking Diversity: Hybridity and Hybrid Language Practices in the Third Space', *Mind, Culture, and Activity*, 6, 286–303.

Gutiérrez, K. D., Bien, A. C., Selland, M. K. and Pierce, D. M. (2011) 'Polylingual and Polycultural Learning Ecologies: Mediating Emergent Academic Literacies for Dual Language Learners', *Journal of Early Childhood Literacy*, 11, 232–261.

DOI: 10.1057/9781137385765

Hall, J. K., Cheng, A. and Carlson, M. T. (2006) 'Reconceptualizing Multicompetence as a Theory of Language Knowledge', *Applied Linguistics*, 27(2), 220–240.

Halliday, M. A. K. (1978) *Language as Social Semiotic* (London: Edward Arnold).

Haugen, E. (1956) *Bilingualism in the Americas: A Bibliography and Research Guide* (Alabama: University of Alabama Press).

Heller, M. (1999) *Linguistic Minorities and Modernity: A Sociolinguistic Ethnography* (London: Longman).

Heller, M. (2007) 'Bilingualism as Ideology and Practice' in M. Heller (ed.) *Bilingualism: A Social Approach* (Basingstoke, Hampshire: Palgrave Macmillan), pp. 1–22.

Heller, M. (2010) *Paths to Postnationalism* (Oxford: Oxford University Press).

Heller, M. and Martin-Jones, M. (2001) *Voices of Authority: Education and Linguistic Difference* (Westport, CT: Ablex).

Hélot, C. and Young, A. (2006) 'Imagining Multilingual Education in France: A Language and Cultural Awareness Project at Primary Level' in O. García, T. Skutnabb-Kangas and M. Torres-Guzmán (eds) *Imagining Multilingual Schools: Languages in Education and Globalization* (Clevedon, UK: Multilingual Matters), pp. 69–90.

Herdina, P. and Jessner, U. (2002) *A Dynamic Model of Multilingualism* (Clevedon, UK: Multilingual Matters).

Hernández, A. E. (2009) 'Language Switching in the Bilingual Brain: What's Next?' *Brain and Language*, 109, 133–140.

Hernández, A. E., Dapretto, M., Mazziotta, J. and Bookheimer, S. (2001) 'Language Switching and Language Representation in Spanish-English Bilinguals: An fMRI Study', *Neuroimage*, 14, 510–520.

Higgins, C. (2009) *English as a Local Language: Post-Colonial Identities and Multilingual Practices* (Bristol, UK: Multilingual Matters).

Hinrichs, L. (2006) *Codeswitching on the Web: English and Jamaican Creole in E-mail Communication* (Amsterdam: John Benjamins).

hooks, bell (1990) *Yearning* (Boston: South End Press).

Hornberger, N. H. (2003) 'Continua of Biliteracy' in N. H. Hornberger (ed.) *Continua of Biliteracy: An Ecological Framework for Educational Policy, Research, and Practice in Multilingual Settings* (Clevedon, UK: Multilingual Matters), pp. 3–34.

DOI: 10.1057/9781137385765

Hornberger, N. H. (2005) 'Opening and Filling Up Implementational and Ideological Spaces in Heritage Language Education', *Modern Language Journal*, 89, 605–609.

Hornberger, N. H. and Chick, K. (2001) 'Co-Constructing School Safetime: Safetalk Practices in Peruvian and South African Classrooms' in M. Heller and M. Martin-Jones (eds) *Voices of Authority. Education and Linguistic Difference* (Westport, CT: Ablex Publishers), pp. 31–56.

Hornberger, N. H. and Link, H. (2012) 'Translanguaging and Transnational Literacies in Multilingual Classrooms: A Bilingual Lens', *International Journal of Bilingual Education and Bilingualism*, 15(3), 261–278.

Hoshino, N. and Thierry G. (2011) 'Language Selection in Bilingual Word Production: Electrophysiological Evidence for Cross-Language Competition', *Brain Research*, 1371, 100–109.

Howatt, A. (1984) *A History of English Language Teaching* (Oxford: Oxford University Press).

Iedema, R. (2003) 'Multimodality, Resemiotization: Extending the Analysis of Discourse as Multi-Semiotic Practice', *Visual Communication*, 2(1), 29–57.

Jacobson, R. (1990) 'Allocating Two Languages as a Key Feature of a Bilingual Methodology' in R. Jacobson and C. Faltis (eds) *Language Distribution Issues in Bilingual Schooling* (Clevedon, UK: Multilingual Matters), pp. 3–17.

Jacobson, R. and Faltis, C. (eds) (1990) *Language Distribution Issues in Bilingual Schooling* (Clevedon, UK: Multilingual Matters).

Jacquemet, M. (2005) 'Transidiomatic Practices: Language and Power in the Age of Globalization', *Language and Communication*, 25, 257–277.

Janks, H. (2000) 'Domination, Access, Diversity and Design: A Synthesis for Critical Literacy Education', *Educational Review*, 52, 175–186.

Javier, R. A. (2007) *The Bilingual Mind. Thinking, Feeling and Speaking in Two Languages* (New York: Springer).

Jewitt, C. (2008) 'Multimodal Discourses Across the Curriculum' in M. Martin-Jones, A. M. de Mejía and N. H. Hornberger (eds) *Encyclopedia of Language and Education, Volume 3. Discourse and Education* (New York: Springer), pp. 357–367.

DOI: 10.1057/9781137385765

Jiménez, R. T., García, G. E. and Pearson, P. D. (1995) 'Three Children, Two Languages, and Strategic Reading: Case Studies in Bilingual/ Monolingual Reading', *American Educational Research Journal*, 32, 31–61.

Joaquin, A. D. L. and Schumann, J. H. (2013) *Exploring Interactional Instinct* (New York: Oxford University Press).

Jørgensen, J. N. (2008) 'Polylingual Languaging Around and Among Children and Adolescents', *International Journal of Multilingualism*, 5(3), 161–176.

Jørgensen, J. N. and Juffermans, K. (2011) *Languaging*, November 2011, http://www.toolkit-online.eu/docs/languaging.html

Juffermans, K. (2011) 'The Old Man and the Letter: Repertoires of Literacy and Langauging in a Modern Multiethnic Gambian Village', *Compare*, 41(2), 165–179.

Kano, N. (2010) Translanguaging as a process and a pedagogical tool for Japanese students in an English writing course in New York. Doctoral dissertation (Teachers College, Columbia University).

Kenner, C. (2004) *Becoming Biliterate: Young Children Learning Different Writing Systems* (Stoke on Trent: Trentham).

Kibler, A. (2010) 'Writing Through Two Languages: First Language Expertise in a Language Minority Classroom', *Journal of Second Language Writing*, 19, 121–142.

Kieffer, M. J., Lesaux, N. K. and Snow, C. E. (2008) 'Promises and Pitfalls: Implications of NCLB for Identifying, Assessing, and Educating English Language Learners' in G. Sunderman (ed.) *Holding NCLB Accountable: Achieving Accountability, Equity, and School Reform* (Thousand Oaks, CA: Corwin Press), pp. 57–74.

Kim, K. H., Relkin, N. R., Lee, K. M. and Hirsch, J. (1997) 'Distinct Cortical Areas Associated with Native and Second Languages', *Nature*, 388, 171–174.

Khubchandani, L. M. (1997) *Revisualizing Boundaries: A Plurilingual Ethos* (New Delhi: Sage).

Kloss, H. and Van Orden, G. (2009) 'Soft-Assembled Mechanisms for the Grand Theory' in J. P. Spencer, M. Thomas and J. McClelland (eds) *Toward a New Grand Theory of Development? Connectionism and Dynamics Systems Theory Reconsidered* (Oxford: Oxford University Press), pp. 253–267.

Kramsch, C. (2009) *The Multilingual Subject* (Oxford: Oxford University Press).

DOI: 10.1057/9781137385765

Kramsch, C. and Whiteside, A. (2008) 'Language Ecology in Multilingual Settings: Towards a Theory of Symbolic Competence', *Applied Linguistics*, 29(4), 645–671.

Krashen, S. (1981) *Second Language Acquisition and Second Language Learning* (Oxford: Pergamon).

Kress, G. (2003) *Literacy in the New Media Age* (London and New York: Routledge).

Kress, G. and Bezemer, J. (2009) 'Writing in a Multimodal World of Representation' in R. Beard, D. Myhill, J. Riley and M. Nystrand (eds) *The Sage Handbook of Writing Development* (London: SAGE Publications Ltd), pp. 167–181.

Kress, G. and van Leeuwen, T. (2001) *Multimodal Discourse* (London: Bloomsbury Academic).

Lam, W. S. E. (2009) 'Multiliteracies on Instant Messaging in Negotiating Local, Translocal, and Transnational Affiliations: A Case of an Adolescent Immigrant', *Reading Research Quarterly*, 44(4), 377–397.

Lambert, W. E. (1974) 'Culture and Language as Factors in Learning and Education' in F. E. Aboud and R. D. Meade (eds) *Cultural Factors in Learning and Education* (Bellingham, Washington: 5th Western Washington Symposium on Learning), pp. 91–122.

Langer, J., Bartolomé, L., Vasquez, O. and Lucas, T. (1990) 'Meaning Construction in School Literacy Tasks: A Study of Bilingual Students', *American Educational Research Journal*, 27(3), 427–471.

Lantolf, J. P. (2000) 'Introducing Sociocultural Theory' in J. P. Lantolf (ed.) *Sociocultural Theory and Second Language Learning* (Oxford: Oxford University Press), pp. 1–26.

Lanza, E. (2007) 'Multilingualism and the Family' in Li Wei and P. Auer (eds) *Handbook of Multilingualism and Multilingual Communication* (Berlin: Mouton de Gruyter), pp. 45–67.

Larsen-Freeman, D. and Cameron, L. (2008) *Complex Systems and Applied Linguistics* (Cambridge: Cambridge University Press).

Lee, J. S., Hill-Bonnet, L. and Gillispie, J. (2008) 'Learning in Two Languages: Interactional Spaces for Becoming Bilingual Speakers', *International Journal of Bilingual Education and Bilingualism*, 11(1), 75–94.

Lee, J. S., Hill-Bonnet, L. and Raley, J. (2011) 'Examining the Effects of Language Brokering on Student Identities and Learning

DOI: 10.1057/9781137385765

Opportunities in Dual Immersion Classrooms', *Journal of Language, Identity, and Education,* 10, 306–326.

Lee, N., Mikesell, L., Joaquin, A. D. J., Mates, A. W. and Schumann, J. H. (2009) *The Interactional Instinct: The Evolution and Acquisition of Language* (New York: Oxford University Press).

Lemke, J. (2002) 'Language Development and Identity: Multiple Timescales in the Social Ecology of Learning' in C. Kramsch (ed.) *Language Acquisition and Language Socialization* (London: Continuum), pp. 68–87.

Lessow-Hurley, J. (1990) *The Foundations of Dual Language Instruction* (New York: Longman).

Lewis, G., Jones, B. and Baker, C. (2012a) 'Translanguaging: Developing its Conceptualisation and Contextualisation', *Educational Research and Evaluation,* 18(7), 655–670.

Lewis, G., Jones, B. and Baker, C. (2012b) 'Translanguaging: Origins and Development from School to Street and Beyond', *Educational Research and Evaluation,* 18(7), 641–654.

Lewis, G., Jones, B. and Baker, C. (2013) '100 Bilingual Lessons: Distributing Two Languages in Classrooms' in C. Abello-Contesse, P. Chandler, M. D. López-Jiménez, M. M. Torreblanca-López and R. Chacón-Beltrán (eds) *Bilingualism and Multiligualism in School Settings* (Bristol: Multilingual Matters).

Lewis, M. Paul, Simons, G. F. and Fennig, C. D. (eds) (2013) *Ethnologue: Languages of the World, Seventeenth Edition* (Dallas, Texas: SIL International), http://www.ethnologue.com

Li Wei (2006) 'Complementary Schools, Past, Present and Future', *Language and Education* 20(1), 76–83.

Li Wei (2011a) 'Multilinguality, Multimodality and Multicompetence: Code- and Mode-Switching by Minority Ethnic Children in Complementary Schools', *Modern Language Journal,* 95(3), 370–384.

Li Wei (2011b) 'Moment Analysis and Translanguaging Space: Discursive Construction of Identities by Multilingual Chinese Youth in Britain', *Journal of Pragmatics,* 43, 1222–1235.

Li Wei (2014) 'Who's Teaching Whom? Co-Learning in Multilingual Classrooms' in S. May (ed.) *The Multilingual Turn: Implications for SLA, TESOL, and Bilingual Education* (New York: Routledge), pp. 167–190.

DOI: 10.1057/9781137385765

Li Wei and Martin, P. (2009) 'Conflicts and Tensions in Classroom Codeswitching', *International Journal of Bilingual Education and Bilingualism*, 12(2), 117–122.

Li Wei and Wu, Chao-Jung (2009) 'Polite Chinese Children Revisited: Creativity and the Use of Codeswitching in the Chinese Complementary School Classroom', *International Journal of Bilingual Education and Bilingualism*, 12(2), 193–212.

Lin, A. M. Y. (1999) 'Doing-English-Lessons in the Reproduction or Transformation of Social Worlds?', *TESOL Quarterly*, 33(3), 393–412.

Lin, A. M. Y. (2013) 'Towards Paradigmatic Change in TESOL Methodologies: Building Plurilingual Pedagogies from the Ground Up', *TESOL Quarterly,* 47(3), 521–545.

Lin, A. M. Y. (forthcoming) 'Hip Hop Heteroglossia as Practice, Pleasure, and Public Pedagogy: Translanguaging in the Lyrical Poetics of "24 Herbs" in Hong Kong' in A. Creese and A. Blackledge (eds) *Heteroglossia as Practice and Pedagogy* (London: Routledge).

Lin, A. M. Y. and Martin, P. W. (eds) (2005) *Decolonisation, Globalization. Language-in-Education Policy and Practice* (Clevedon, UK: Multilingual Matters).

Lindholm-Leary, K. (2001) *Dual Language Education* (Clevedon, UK: Multilingual Matters).

Lindholm-Leary, K. (2006) 'What are the Most Effective Kinds of Programs for English Language Learners?' in E. Hamayan and R. Freeman (eds) *English Language Learners at School* (Philadelphia: Caslon), pp. 64–85.

Linguistic Society of America (1995) *LSA Statement on Language Rights*, 15 November 1995, Posted by Geoffrey Numberg, http://www.smo.uhi.ac.uk/saoghal/mion-chanain/LSA_statement.txt

Macaro, E. (2001) 'Analysing Student Teachers' Codeswitching in Foreign Language Classrooms: Theories and Decision-Making', *The Modern Language Journal*, 85(4), 531–48.

Macaro, E. (2006) 'Codeswitching in the L2 Classroom: A Communication and Learning Strategy' in Llurda, E. *Non-Native Language Teachers: Perceptions, Challenges and Contributions to the Profession* (New York: Springer), pp. 63–84.

Makoni, B. and Makoni, S. (2010) 'Multilingual Discourses on Wheels and Public English in Africa. A Case for Vague Linguistique' in J. Maybin and J. Swaan (eds) *Routledge Companion to English Language Studies* (New York: Routledge), pp. 258–270.

DOI: 10.1057/9781137385765

Makoni, S. and Pennycook, A. (2007) *Disinventing and Reconstituting Languages* (Clevedon, UK: Multilingual Matters).

Makoni, S., Makoni, B., Abdelhay, A. and Mashiri, P. (2012) 'Colonial and Post-Colonial Language Policies in Africa: Historical and Emerging Landscapes' in Spolsky, B. *Language Policy* (Oxford: Oxford University Press), pp. 523–543.

Manyak, P. (2000) 'Borderlands Literacy in a Primary-Grade Immersion Class' in T. Shanahan and F. Rodriguez-Brown (eds) *Forty-Ninth Yearbook of the National Reading Conference* (Chicago, IL: National Reading Conference), pp. 91–108.

Manyack, P. (2004) 'What Did She Say? Translation in a Primary-Grade English Immersion Class', *Multicultural Perspectives*, 6(1), 12–18.

Martin, P. (2005) '"Safe" Language Practices in Two Rural Schools in Malaysia: Tensions Between Policy and Practice' in A. M. Y. Lin and P. W. Martin (eds) *Decolonisation, Globalisation. Language-in-Education Policy and Practice* (Clevedon, UK: Multilingual Matters), pp. 74–974.

Martín-Beltrán, M. (2010) 'The Two Way Language Bridge: Co-Constructing Bilingual Language Learning Opportunities', *Modern Language Journal*, 94(ii), 254–277.

Martin-Jones, M. (1995) 'Code-Switching in the Classroom: Two Decades of Research' in L. Milroy and P. Muysken (eds) *One Speaker, Two Languages: Cross-Disciplinary Perspectives on Code-Switching* (Cambridge, UK: Cambridge University Press), pp. 90–111.

Martin-Jones, M. and Jones, K. (eds) (2001) *Multilingual Literacies: Reading and Writing Different Worlds* (Amsterdam: Benjamins).

Martínez, R. A. (2010) 'Spanglish As Literacy Tool: Toward an Understanding of the Potential Role of Spanish-English Code-Switching in the Development of Academic Literacy', *Research in the Teaching of English*, 45(2), 124–149.

Martínez-Roldán, C. and Sayer, P. (2006) 'Reading through Linguistic Borderlands: Latino Students' Transactions with Narrative Texts', *Journal of Early Childhood Literacy*, 6, 293–322.

Maturana, H. and Varela, F. (1998) [1st edn 1973, rev. edn of 1987] *The Tree of Knowledge. The Biological Roots of Human Understanding* (Boston and London: Shambhala).

May, S. (ed.) (2013) *The Multilingual Turn: Implications for SLA, TESOL, and Bilingual Education* (New York: Routledge).

DOI: 10.1057/9781137385765

Mazak, C. M. and Herbas-Donoso, C. (2013) Classroom Translanguaging Practices and Language Ideologies in Puerto Rican University Science Education (Unpublished Manuscript).

Menezes de Souza, L. M. (2007) 'Entering a Culture Quietly: Writing and Cultural Survival in Indigenous Education in Brazil' in S. Makoni and A. Pennycook (eds) *Disinventing and Reconstituting Languages* (Clevedon, UK: Multilingual Matters), pp. 135–169.

Menken, K. and García, O. (eds) (2010) *Negotiating Language Policies in Schools: Educators as Policymakers* (New York: Routledge).

Merritt, M. (1992) 'Socialising Multilingualism: Determinants of Codeswitching in Kenyan Primary Classrooms', *Journal of Multilingual and Multicultural Development*, 13(1&2), 103–121.

Michael-Luna, S. and Canagarajah, A. S. (2007) 'Multilingual Academic Literacies: Pedagogical Foundations for Code Meshing in Primary and Higher Education', *Journal of Applied Linguistics*, 4(1), 55–77.

Michaels, S. (2005) 'Can the Intellectual Affordances of Working-Class Storytelling be Leveraged in School?' *Human Development*, 48, 136–145.

Mignolo, W. (2000) *Local Histories/Global Designs. Coloniality, Subaltern Knowledges, and Border Thinking* (Princeton: Princeton University Press).

Moje, E. B., McIntosh Ciechanowski, K., Kramer, K., Ellis, L., Carrillo, R. and Collazo, T. (2004) 'Working Toward Third Space in Content Area Literacy: An Examination of Everyday Funds of Knowledge and Discourse', *Reading Research Quarterly*, 39(1), 38–70.

Moll, L. C, Díaz, S., Estrada, E. and Lopes, L. (1992) 'Making Contexts: The Social Construction of Lessons in Two Languages' in M. Saravia-Shore and S. F. Arvizu (eds) *Cross-Cultural Literacy: Ethnographies of Communication in Multiethnic Classrooms* (New York: Garland), pp. 339–366.

Møller, J. S. (2008) 'Polylingual Performance Among Turkish-Danes in Late-Modern Copenhagen', *International Journal of Multilingualism*, 5(3), 217–237.

Møller, J. S. and Jørgensen, J. N. (2009) 'From Language to Languaging: Changing Relations Between Humans and Linguistic Features', *Acta Linguistica Hafniensia*, 41, 143–166.

Montes-Alcalá, C. (2007) 'Blogging in Two Languages: Code-Switching in Bilingual Blogs' in J. Holmquist, A. Lorenzino and L. Sayahi (eds) *Selected Proceedings of the Third Workshop on Spanish Sociolinguistics* (Somerville, MA: Cascadilla), pp. 162–170.

DOI: 10.1057/9781137385765

Morrell, E. (2008) *Critical Literacy and Urban Youth: Pedagogies of Access, Dissent, and Liberation* (London: Routledge).

Morris, P. (1994) *The Bakhtin Reader: Selected Writings of Bakhtin, Medvedev, Voloshinov* (London: Arnold).

Myers-Scotton, C. (1993) *Dueling Languages: Grammatical Structure in Codeswitching* (Oxford: Carlendon Press).

Namy, L. L. and Waxman, S. R. (1998) 'Words and Gestures: Infants' Interpretations of Different Forms of Symbolic Reference', *Child Development*, 69(2), 295–308.

Ngugi wa Thiong'o (1986) *Decolonising the African Mind: The Politics of Language in African Literature* (London: James Currey Ltd).

Nicholas, H. and Starks, D. (2014) *Languge Education and Applied Linguistics: Multiplicity as a Framework for Bridging the Two Fields* (New York: Routledge).

Norton, B. (2000) *Identity and Language Learning: Gender, Ethnicity and Educational Change* (Harlow, UK: Longman).

Norris, S. (2004). *Analyzing Multimodal Interaction: A Methodological Framework* (London: Routledge).

Orellana, M. F. (2009) *Translating Childhoods: Immigrant Youth, Language, and Culture* (New Brunswick, NJ: Rutgers University Press).

Orellana, M. F. and Reynolds, J. (2008) 'Cultural Modeling: Leveraging Bilingual Skills for School Paraphrasing Tasks', *Reading Research Quarterly*, 43(1), 48–65.

Ortiz, F. (1940/1978) *Contrapunteo cubano del tabaco y el azúcar [Tobacco and Sugar: A Cuban Counter Point]* (Caracas: Biblioteca Ayacucho).

Otheguy, R. and Stern, N. (2010) 'On So-Called Spanglish', *International Journal of Bilingualism*, 15(1), 85–100.

Otsuji, E. and Pennycook, A. (2010) 'Metrolingualism: Fixity, Fluidity and Language in Flux', *International Journal of Multilingualism*, 7(3), 240–254.

Otsuji, E. and Pennycook, A. (2011) 'Social Inclusion and Metrolingual Practices', *International Journal of Bilingual Education and Bilingualism*, 14(4), 413–426.

Pahl, K. (2004) 'Narratives, Artifacts and Cultural Identities: An Ethnographic Study of Communicative Practices in Homes', *Linguistics and Education*, 15, 339–358.

Pahl, K. and Roswell, J. (2006) 'Introduction' in K. Pahl and J. Rowsell (eds) *Travel Notes from the New Literacy Studies* (Clevedon, UK: Multilingual Matters).

DOI: 10.1057/9781137385765

Palmer, D. (2008) 'Diversity Up Close: Building Alternative Discourses in the Dual Immersion Classroom' in T. Fortune and D. Tedick (eds) *Pathways to Multilingualism: Evolving Perspectives on Immersion Education* (London, UK: Multilingual Matters), pp. 97–116.

Palmer, D. and Martínez, R. A. (2013) 'Teacher Agency in Bilingual Spaces: A Fresh Look at Preparing Teachers to Educate Latina/o Bilingual Children', *Review of Research in Education*, 37, 269–297.

Paris, S. and Paris, A. (2001) 'Classroom Applications of Research on Self-Regulated Learning', *Educational Psychologist*, 36(2), 89–101.

Pavlenko, A. (2006) *Bilingual Minds. Emotional Experience, Expression and Representation* (Clevedon, UK: Multilingual Matters).

Pennycook, A. (2010) *Language as a Local Practice* (London and New York: Routledge).

Pinker, S. (1994) *The Language Instinct* (London: Penguin).

Plester, B., Lerkkanen, M.-K., Linjama, L. J., Rasku-Puttonen, H. and Littleton, K. (2011) 'Finnish and UK English Pre-Teen Children's Text Message Language and its Relationship with their Literacy Skills', *Journal of Computer Assisted Learning*, 27(1), 37–48.

Pratt, M. L. (1991) 'Arts of the Contact Zone', *Profession*, 91, 33–40.

Rampton, B. (1995) *Crossing: Language and Ethnicity Among Adolescents* (London, UK: Longman).

Reyes, M. de la Luz (2001) 'Unleashing Possibilities: Biliteracy in the Primary Grades' in M. de la Luz Reyes and J. J. Halcón (eds) *The Best for Our Children. Critical Perspectives on Literacy for Latino Students* (New York: Teachers College Press), pp. 96–121.

Roeper, T. (1999) 'Universal Bilingualism', *Bilingualism Language and Cognition*, 2, 169–186.

Rosa, J. D. (2010) Looking Like a Language, Sounding Like a Race: Making Latin@ Panethnicity and Managing American Anxieties, Unpublished Doctoral Dissertation (University of Chicago).

Rubagumya, C. M. (ed.) (1994) *Teaching and Researching Language in African Classrooms* (Clevedon, UK: Multilingual Matters).

Rubdy, R. (2005) 'Remaking Singapore for the New Age: Official Ideology and the Realities of Practice in Language-in-Education' in A. M. Y. Lin and P. W. Martin (eds) *Decolonisation, Globalization. Language-in-Education Policy and Practice* (Clevedon, UK: Multilingual Matters), pp. 55–73.

Sánchez, P. (2007) 'Cultural Authenticity and Transnational Latina Youth', *Linguistics and Education*, 18, 258–282.

DOI: 10.1057/9781137385765

Saxena, M. (2006) 'Multilingual and Multicultural Identities in Brunei Darussalam' in A. B. M. Tsui and J. Tollefson (eds) *Language Policy, Culture and Identity in Asian Contexts* (Mahwah, NJ: Lawrence Erlbaum), pp. 262–303.

Sayer, P. (2008) 'Demystifying Language Mixing: Spanglish in School', *Journal of Latinos and Education*, 7(2), 94–112.

Sayer, P. (2013) 'Translanguaging, TexMex, and Bilingual Pedagogy: Emergent Bilinguals Learning through the Vernacular', *TESOL Quarterly*, 47(1), 63–88.

Schechter, S. R. and Cummins, J. (eds) (2003) *Multilingual Education in Practice: Using Diversity as a Resource* (Portsmouth, NH: Heinemann).

Scollon, R. and Scollon, S. W. (2004) *Nexus Analysis: Discourse and the Emerging Internet* (New York: Routledge).

Sebba, M. (2012) 'Researching and Theorizing Multilingual Texts' in M. Sebba (ed.) *Language Mixing and Code-Switching in Writing: Approaches to Mixed Language Written Discourse* (New York: Routledge), pp. 1–26.

Sebba, M., Mahootian, S. and Jonsson, C. (eds) (2011) 'Language Mixing and Code-Switching in Writing', *Approaches to Mixed Language Written Discourse* (New York: Longman).

Shanker, S. and King, B. (2002) 'The Emergence of a New Paradigm in Ape Language Research', *Behavioral and Brain Sciences*, 25(5), 605–656.

Shirazi, R. and Borjian, M. (2013) 'Persian Bilingual and Community Education Among Iranian-Americans in New York City' in O. García, Z. Zakharia and B. Otcu (eds) (2013) *Bilingual Community Education for American Children: Beyond Heritage Languages in a Global City* (Bristol, UK: Multilingual Matters), pp. 154–168.

Shohamy, E. (2001) *The Power of Tests: A Critical Perspective on the Uses of Language Tests* (Harlow, UK: Longman).

Shohamy, E. (2006) *Language Policy: Hidden Agendas and New Approaches* (London, UK: Routledge).

Shohamy, E. (2011) 'Assessing Multilingual Competencies: Assessing Construct Valid Assessment Policies', *The Modern Language Journal*, 95(iii), 418–429.

Shohamy, E. and Gorter, D. (eds) (2009) *Linguistic Landscape: Expanding the Scenery* (London: Rutledge).

Shohamy, E., Ben Rafael, E. and Barni, C. (eds) (2010) *Linguistic Landscape in the City* (Bristol: Multilingual Matters).

Silverstein, M. (1996) '"Monoglot" Standard in America: Standardization and Metaphors of Linguistic Hegemony', in D.

DOI: 10.1057/9781137385765

Brenneis and
R. Macauley (eds) *The Matrix of Language: Contemporary Linguistic Anthropology* (Boulder, CO: Westview Press), pp. 284–306.

Skutnabb-Kangas, T. (2000) *Linguistic Genocide in Education – or Worldwide Diversity and Human Rights?* (Mahwah, NJ: Lawrence Erlbaum).

Soja, E. W. (1996) *Thirdspace: Journeys to Los Angeles and Other Real-and-Imagined Places* (Malden, MA and Oxford: Blackwell).

Sollors, W. (2009) 'Multilingualism in the United States: A Less Well-Known Source of Vitalityin American Culture as an Issue of Social Justice and of Historical Memory', *Nanzan Review of American Studies*, 31, 59–75.

Stavans, I. (2000) 'The Gravitas of Spanglish', *Chronicle of Higher Education*, 13 October 2000, B7.

Stavans, I. (2003) *Spanglish: The Making of a New American Language* (New York: Rayo).

Storch, N. and Wigglesworth, G. (2003) 'Is There a Role for the Use of the L1 in an L2 Setting?' *TESOL Quarterly*, 37(4), 760–770.

Street, B. (1993) *Cross-Cultural Approaches To Literacy* (Cambridge: Cambridge University Press).

Swain, M. (2000) 'The Output Hypothesis and Beyond: Mediating Acquisition Through Collaborative Dialogue' in J. Lantolf (ed.) *Sociocultural Theory and Second Language Learning* (Oxford: Oxford University Press), pp. 97–114.

Swain, M. (2006) 'Languaging, Agency and Collaboration in Advanced Second Language Learning' in H. Byrnes (ed.) *Advanced Language Learning: The Contributions of Halliday and Vygotsky* (London: Continuum), pp. 95–108.

Swain, M. and Deters, P. (2007) ' "New" Mainstream SLA Theory: Expanded and Enriched', *The Modern Language Journal*, 91, 820–836.

Swain, M. and Lapkin, S. (1998) 'Interaction and Second Language Learning: Two Adolescent French Immersion Students Working Together' *Modern Language Journal*, 82, 320–337.

Swain, M. and Lapkin, S. (2000) 'Task-Based Second Language Learning: The Uses of the First Language', *Language Teaching Research*, 4(3), 251–274.

The "Five Graces Group", Beckner, C., Blythe, R., Bybee, J., Christiansen, M. H., Croft, W., Ellis, N. C., Holland, J., Ke, J., Larsen-Freeman,

DOI: 10.1057/9781137385765

D. and Schoenemann, T. (2009) 'Language Is a Complex Adaptive System: Position Paper', *Language Learning*, 59, 1–26.

Thierry, G., Athanasopoulos A., Wiggett A., Dering B. and Kuipers J. R. (2009) 'Unconscious effects of Language-Specific Terminology On Preattentive Color Perception', *Proceedings of the National Academy of Science* (U.S.A.), 106, 4567–4570.

Thierry, G. and Wu, Y. J. (2007) 'Brain Potentials Reveal Unconscious Translation During Foreign-Language Comprehension', *PNAS*, 104(30), 12530–12535.

Tomasello, M. (2003) *Constructing a Language: A Usage-Based Theory of Language Acquisition* (Cambridge, MA: Harvard University Press).

Tomasello, M. (2008) *Origins of Human Communication* (Cambridge, MA: MIT Press).

Turvey, M. T. and Carello, C. (1981) 'Cognition: The View from Ecological Realism', *Cognition*, 10(1–3), 313–321.

US Census Bureau (2007) *Language Use in the United States: 2007*, http://www.census.gov/hhes/socdemo/language/data/acs/ACS-12.pdf

US Census Bureau (2009) *American Community Survey: 2009*.

Vertovec, S. (2007) 'Super-Diversity and Its Implications', *Ethnic and Racial Studies*, 30(6), 1024–1054.

Velasco, P. and García, O. (2013) Translanguaging and the Writing of Bilingual Learners (Unpublished manuscript).

Vološinov, V. N. (1929/1973) *Marxism and the Philosophy of Language* [Original publication in Russian 1929, English translation by L. Matejka and I. R. Titunik, 1973] (Cambridge, MA: Harvard University Press).

Vygotsky, L. S. (1978) *Mind and Society* (Cambridge, MA: Harvard University Press).

Weinreich, U. (1953/1974) *Languages in Contact, Findings and Problems* (The Hague: Mouton).

Williams, C. (1994) *Arfarniad o Ddulliau Dysgu ac Addysgu yng Nghyd-destun Addysg Uwchradd Ddwyieithog*, [An evaluation of teaching and learning methods in the context of bilingual secondary education]. Unpublished Doctoral Thesis (University of Wales, Bangor).

Williams, C. (1996) 'Secondary Education: Teaching in the bilingual situation' in C. Williams, G. Lewis and C. Baker (eds) *The Language Policy: Taking Stock* (Llangefni, UK: CAI), pp. 39–78.

Williams, C. (2002) *Ennill Iaith: Astudiaeth o Sefyllfa Drochi yn 11-16 Oed* [*A Language Gained: A Study of Language Immersion at 11-16 Years of*

DOI: 10.1057/9781137385765

Age] (Bangor, UK: School of Education), http://www.bangor.ac.uk/addysg/publictions/Ennill_Iaith.pdf

Williams, C. (2012) *The National Immersion Scheme Guidance for Teachers on Subject Language Threshold: Accelerating the Process of Reaching the Threshold* (Bangor, Wales: The Welsh Language Board).

Woolard, K. (1998) 'Language Ideology as a Field of Inquiry' in B. Schieffelin, K. Woolard and P. Kroskrity (eds) *Language Ideologies: Practice and Theory* (New York: Oxford University Press), pp. 3–49.

Wu, Y. J. and Thierry, G. (2010) 'Investigating Bilingual Processing: The Neglected Role of Language Processing Contexts', *Frontiers in Psychology*, 1, 178.

Yu, L. (2001) 'Communicative Language Teaching in China: Progress and Resistance' *TESOL Quarterly*, 35(1), 194–198.

Zentella, A. C. (1997) *Growing Up Bilingual. Puerto Rican Children in New York* (Malden, MA: Wiley/Blackwell).

DOI: 10.1057/9781137385765

Index

additive bilingualism, 12, 13, 14,
    16, 20, 43, 49, 50, 58
agency, 9, 43, 74, 75, 85, 108
Anzaldúa, Gloria, 43
assessment, 56, 74, 117,
    132, 133
Auer, Peter, 12
autopoeisis, 7, 8

Baetens Beardsmore, Hugo,
    49, 70
Bailey, Benjamin, 36
Baker, Colin, 20, 48, 64, 65,
    81, 92
Bakhtin, Mikhail, 7, 36, 37, 94
Becker, A.L., 8, 9, 40, 79
Bialystok, Ellen, 15
bilanguaging, 40
bilingual education, 48–52
    bilingual community
        education, 51
    CLIL, 76
    developmental, 50
    dual language or dual
        immersion, 55, 58, 60, 82
    dynamic bi/plurilingual, 76
    immersion, 50
    immersion revitalization, 50
    maintenance, 49
    multiple multilingual
        education, 51
    prestigious, 50
    transitional, 49
biliteracy, 61, 62, 66

Blackledge, Adrian, 20,
    22, 51, 58, 66, 89,
    92, 115, 116
Blommaert, Jan, 9
Borges, Jorge Luis, 25, 68, 77
Bourdieu, Pierre, 47, 79

Canagarajah, Suresh, 9, 10, 17,
    20, 21, 39, 40, 85, 86, 91,
    108, 131, 143
Cenoz, Jasone, 48, 49, 51, 70
Chinese, 6, 7, 17, 33, 34,
    35, 41, 59, 67, 105, 106,
    112, 113, 114
Chomsky, Noam, 6, 7, 9, 12,
    17, 30
CLIL, 76
Clyne, Michael, 16
codemeshing, 36, 39, 40, 85,
    108
code-switching, 12, 13, 22, 52,
    53, 57, 58, 60, 62, 65, 76
cognition, 3, 13, 16, 31, 40, 42,
    53, 61, 64, 79
community language
    schools, 50
Cook, Vivian, 10, 11, 21
creativity, 24, 25, 29, 30, 31, 32,
    36, 42, 52, 66, 67, 68, 74,
    85, 86
Creese, Angela, 20, 22, 51, 57,
    58, 66, 89, 92, 115, 116
criticality, 3, 24, 29, 42, 66, 67,
    68, 74, 85, 86

DOI: 10.1057/9781137385765

Made in the USA
Middletown, DE
30 November 2017